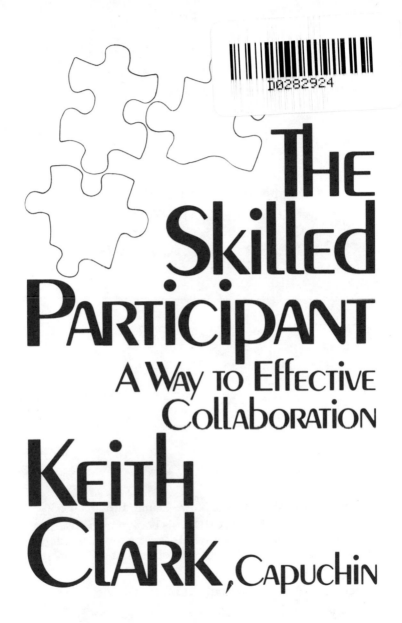

The
Skilled
Participant
A Way to Effective Collaboration

Keith
Clark, Capuchin

AVE MARIA PRESS Notre Dame, IN 46556

Other books by Keith Clark, Capuchin
MAKE SPACE, MAKE SYMBOLS
AN EXPERIENCE OF CELIBACY
BEING SEXUAL . . . AND CELIBATE

© 1988 by Ave Maria Press, Notre Dame, Indiana 46556

International Standard Book Number: 0-87793-387-1

Library of Congress Catalog Card Number: 88-71324

Printed and bound in the United States of America.

Contents

For F.D., a skilled participant.

___Introduction___

This book was conceived in guilt and born of frustration.

Even as I was writing *Being Sexual . . . and Celibate* (Ave Maria Press, 1986), part of my consciousness chided me for so strongly advocating the development of *self-awareness, self-disclosure* and *hearing* while failing to offer any suggestion for attaining those skills. I have continued to chide myself for that failure. This book is my attempt to offer some concrete suggestions and theoretical basis for those skills that allow individuals to connect with each other personally.

My frustration is with "group work." I have facilitated several groups in learning how to communicate better with each other, setting group goals and resolving conflict within the group. I have been a member of several groups in which an outside facilitator helped us to set yearly goals for ourselves, to understand better our interaction and to set priorities for our work. My experience of being both an outside facilitator and a member of a group facilitated by someone who is not a regular member have led me to conclude that having an outside facilitator offers little lasting benefit to a group.

Part of the reason is that the group relies on the facilitator's ability to "make us do something" or to "do something for us." When the facilitator leaves, the participants may assume that the departing facilitator has absconded with the skill on which the group relied. The participants are liable to accept their status quo as an inevitable situation which they are powerless to change.

Not only difficult or unpleasant situations appear inevitable. When a group experiences pleasant and profitable situations, members tell themselves "We're just lucky." "Things are going well," they say. They accept it as somehow destined, beyond their control, or the product of chance.

In contrast, my growing convictions are these:

1. Nothing ever just happens, either for good or for ill; all situations result from someone's behavior, whether or not that person intended the results.
2. Outside facilitation may profit a group if the outsider provides a method for dealing with an issue or encourages the group to do what they already wanted to do and could have done without the outsider.
3. On-going groups will experience satisfaction as a group in almost direct proportion to the presence of participants skilled at self-awareness, self-disclosure and hearing.
4. Therefore, the best thing I can do as a member of any group is to develop my own personal skill at self-awareness, self-disclosure and hearing; becoming a skilled participant will benefit any group.

I have been a member of several groups and I think of these as I solidify my convictions: family, religious community, church-related groups, educational groups and groups of administrators. In my opinion, however, what is true of these groups is true of all groups. A friend who read part of an early draft of this book said to me, ''Do you realize the importance these ideas could have for marriage?'' I think I realize the importance of these ideas for the interaction of spouses, of parents and children, for corporate board meetings, for church pastoral councils and for religious communities. Any gathering can benefit from a number of skilled participants, people good at self-awareness, self-disclosure and hearing.

At an age more advanced than I considered optimal for the task, I was assigned to a religious high school. Part of my role there involved listening to individual students. Interviews frequently began like this:

''How are you?''

''Fine. Things are going well so far this year.''

''What's going well?''

''Oh, studies. I'm getting good grades. And our class seems to be pulling together quite a bit better than last year. I'm getting along better with my friends.''

''What are you doing differently than you did last year?''

''Huh?!''

''I don't believe things just go well. If things are going well, that means you're doing something right. If you can figure out what you're doing right, then you can continue the behavior and repeat it in other circumstances and situations and make them go well too.''

7

During the first few months, I was surprised at how readily the kids could identify what they were doing right, what others were doing right and how their satisfying situation was the result of their behavior. I'm no longer surprised. I now anticipate that the kid who initially felt lucky because "things are going well" will on second thought take some responsibility for doing something right.

People enter into married partnerships as individuals. Parents and children relate as individuals. Individuals make up religious communities, boards of directors, diocesan pastoral councils, faculties of schools and yes, even a high school sophomore class.

Spouses, colleagues, classmates—the words themselves imply being joined with others. The success of any joint venture depends on the skills of the individuals. Structures, commitments, accidents of history and even necessity may bring and keep people together, but this alone will not assure their performance. Structures will be neglected, commitments will become strained, necessity will be resented and eventually overcome, unless the members of a group experience the satisfaction of being personally connected with each other.

Groups that experience personal connectedness quite readily devise and operate within structures which serve them. When the structures fail to serve, they are examined and changed. Commitments of individuals to the other members of the group and to the joint enterprise they have undertaken are stronger than the required compliance with agreed-upon structures and roles. The group celebrates the circumstances that brought them together as unsought and undeserved blessings. They recognize and embrace

8

the benefits of staying together as necessary for each one's personal integrity. The skilled participant contributes to and is personally supported by all the elements which bring and keep a group together.

The ideas this book contains will help people relate to each other in any group situation. It is not, however, a book on "group work." I don't intend that this book be used by a group trying to improve interaction among its members. This is a book about developing personal abilities that will enable an individual to be a skilled participant in any group.

Those who know me only from having read previous books may be surprised that the topic of this book is not more religious. I have resisted the urge to "baptize" the dynamics of human interaction with liberal references to church-related events or with quotations and examples from the bible. I don't think the dynamics of human interaction need to be justified religiously. They were Christened when God came among us in human form.

I have written previously about praying, sexuality and celibacy. I believe that people will experience benefit in all three of these areas of human life if they develop the skills required to be a skilled participant. Whether in relationship to God or to other human beings, my sense of connectedness increases immensely when I am reasonably skilled at self-awareness, self-disclosure and hearing.

One

Out of Isolation

My friend Jerry and I have spent many hours in conversation trying to sort out the ways feelings, motivations, attitudes and perceptions interacted within us to induce us to choose the behaviors we did. We assumed if we could understand ourselves more clearly, we could also understand others with increased clarity.

We took delight in our increasing self-awareness and in our disclosing to each other what we were becoming aware of. We had set aside an evening each month just to talk at his house or mine. We began by speaking about what one or both of us had experienced, how we felt about it, what we thought about it, how things might be different and how we wanted to live. Our discussions had no order and no point at which we told ourselves we needed to arrive. We shared a two or three or even four hour session of self-awareness, self-disclosure and hearing one another. Those times became the least pragmatic yet most cherished hours of those years, and the time I most anticipated.

In the course of those evening discussions we turned our attention eventually to our relationship with each other and how it had developed. From what we remembered of our earlier experiences, it appeared that we had done basically what we were doing now in our monthly get-togethers, but in a less systematic and deliberate way. We had felt safe enough to disclose to each other our private interior worlds—those parts of our inner worlds we were proud of and those parts about which we entertained doubts.

We knew we had become friends through significant conversations shared over the years. We knew we could speak to each other very freely. During one of our evening talks I realized and said to Jerry, "When I'm with you my self-awareness and my self-disclosure are almost simultaneous. I am willing to say to you whatever comes into my consciousness without first trying to censor or perfect it." From that kind of realization, we eventually concluded that the connectedness, friendship and intimacy we experienced arose because of the dynamics of self-awareness, self-disclosure and hearing. We supposed and theorized that the same is true of other people.

I once heard a lecturer say, "Every person who appears on the horizon of my life does so as a stranger to my unique experience." That rang true. If I am going to make contact with those strangers and connect with them, both they and I are going to have to bridge the gulf that exists between us by reason of the uniqueness of our experiences. Those experiences may be

11

similar, but we will never know that if we don't manage to overcome the fact that none of us has experienced precisely what another has.

Through the disclosure of my unique experience another can come to know whether or not his or her experience is similar to mine. If the other person hears the disclosure of my awareness of what I have experienced, my disclosure may put the other in touch with his or her own unique experience. In that process we may each come to know that, for all our uniqueness, we are not alone. Whether the experiences disclosed by each of us are similar or very different doesn't matter at all. What matters is that we have contacted each other and have made a connection across the gulf that made us strangers.

In order for this kind of connectedness to occur between us, we both need some considerable skill in self-awareness, self-disclosure and hearing. Developing and exercising those skills allow for intimacy between two otherwise lonely and isolated people. We still remain individual and unique; but we have connected personally.

Jerry and I hypothesized that whatever could facilitate the development and exercise of skills at self-awareness, self-disclosure and hearing would be an aid in perfecting those behaviors that bring about the personal connectedness all people need and healthy people crave.

Craving and needing intimacy doesn't bring it about. People frequently settle for relating to other human beings in ways other than intimacy.

Dominating others and telling oneself that all others exist only in relationship to me, and that they must be kept in their place, is one way I might relate to other human beings. Dominance may keep the relationship clearly defined and may gain for the one who dominates the recognition and subservient behavior he or she desires from others. But dominance is not personally satisfying, whether we experience it politically, sexually, racially or in the one-up-man-ship which often occurs in casual conversation. Neither the dominant nor the subservient one is personally nourished, no matter how fervently either of them tries to maintain the relationship.

Manipulating people is a way of relating to them that establishes clear lines of connectedness—clear to the manipulator, but not to the ones being manipulated. The manipulator gets what he or she wants, but the ones being manipulated don't know they are giving what the manipulator wants. This is not satisfying to the manipulator, because he or she always has to be "fixing" the relationship by further schemes to "get them to" do what seems required. It is not satisfying for the ones who are manipulated, because they are not giving by choice what the manipulator wants.

Romantic and genital sexual encounters may provide gratification, but they alone will not provide the satisfaction and fulfillment of the human need for intimacy.

Success, position, prestige and a lot of other things can serve as distractions—even prolonged distractions—from one's need for personal connections with others. But they can neither replace nor fulfill one's need for intimacy. Failing to achieve intimacy, human beings remain isolated from one another.

People who need and crave intimacy settle for less because they do not know how to develop the skills at self-awareness, self-disclosure and hearing that will give rise to intimacy in their lives. Only intimate personal relationships can lead people out of the isolation imposed by their uniqueness. Believing this I have tried to discover a method that would help me increase the clarity of my self-awareness, the accuracy of my self-disclosure and the acuteness of my hearing.

With the help of two friends, I have found and created such a method, which I call the "Sometimes Useful Tool." With it I am more able to recognize what goes on inside of me—to distinguish my perception from my interpretation of what I perceive, to distinguish my feelings from my opinion. At times I have been more able to disclose my unique inner experience accurately. This tool has helped me recognize that I will be happier when I choose my behavior on the basis of what I want, rather than allowing myself to be manipulated into choosing my behavior on the basis of my feelings alone. It has helped me take responsibility for my own behavior and its consequences.

Not only in conversations with friends has the "Sometimes Useful Tool" proved helpful. In discussing a variety of topics in many situations—most of them job-related in an institutional church setting—I believe I have been able to contribute to the understanding of the topics. When I spoke I distinguished my perception from my interpretation and both of these from my feelings. Being aware of what I wanted from situations has enabled me to ask for it directly rather than to manipulate discussions and those involved in them in order to get what I wanted, perhaps without knowing I wanted anything or was behaving manipulatively.

Because connecting personally with others is so

important, the "Sometimes Useful Tool" can benefit anyone who wants to be a skilled participant.

It has importance for married life, friendship, religious life, ministry within the church and, I believe, in business and even international relations. I have in mind and direct this book toward those who spend a large part of their time and energy interacting with others in an institutional setting within the church. I'll leave it to others to discover what application the "Sometimes Useful Tool" has beyond the church.

In almost all human interaction and verbal exchange an analysis of a situation takes place, an emotional reaction to that analysis sets in, and some strategy for response is formulated. It is helpful to be clear about what one is analyzing and from what basis or biases the analysis is being done. It is helpful to recognize and to distinguish the analysis from the emotional reaction, and to distinguish these things from the response.

The "Sometimes Useful Tool" represents something that goes on first inside of us. We sort out our awareness of our inner experience and what we may want to disclose of that. It also represents what we externalize in our disclosure of ourselves. When we think and speak we utilize it as an internal entity. When we listen to others it serves as a format into which we can fit what we hear; we then use it as a tool to sort out what comes to us from outside ourselves.

The "Sometimes Useful Tool" will not lead people out of isolation. But for those who have the will to connect with other people, the tool can be useful in achieving what they desire.

_____ Two _____

The Sometimes Useful Tool

At the time Jerry and I were trying to develop a schema of the inner psychic workings that induced people to behave as they did, we both had jobs we thought demanded that we understand as fully as we could the people we tried to serve. We began with the assumption that the path to understanding others was to be found in understanding ourselves. We could only speculate about what went on inside of others; our own inner workings we could examine and talk about with each other, holding up to the other our perception of ourselves and giving the other access to the data of our own mental processes.

As months passed we put the various elements into many a schema and tested those diagrams and outlines against what we knew we had experienced. None satisfied us completely.

During that time I stopped unannounced at the

University of Notre Dame to visit another friend, Marlene. Yes, she would be free for dinner later if I'd be willing to wait until she finished an informal early evening presentation she was scheduled to make to a group of men and women religious leaders. Why didn't I just accompany her to the apartment where the fifteen or so people were gathering for her presentation?

What she did and said that evening provided the schema Jerry and I had been trying for months to construct. Without notes other than five 8½'' by 11'' papers, each with one word written on it, Marlene narrated a fictitious story as an enlightening example of what she was presenting. This was my introduction to what I have since come to call the ''Sometimes Useful Tool.''

''People tend to think an event causes them to feel a certain way,'' Marlene began, ''and because people feel the way they do, they think they behave a certain way—even that they have to behave the way they do.''

Marlene placed three sheets of paper side-by-side on the floor. On the first was printed the word *EVENT*, on the second *FEELING* and on the third *BEHAVIOR*.

''For instance, if I were standing with a friend in the foyer of an auditorium and a man bumped into me and stepped squarely on my foot, I might feel very annoyed and turn to him and say, 'Why don't you watch where you're going?!' It would seem very automatic: the event—having my foot stepped on—caused the feeling—annoyance—which in turn caused me to behave as I did—to speak harshly to the man.

''If, however, just after I had spoken harshly to the person who had stepped on my foot, I saw that he was wearing dark glasses and held a white cane in his hand, I might immediately regret my behavior. Seeing the glasses and cane I'd have an entirely different set of feelings which would prompt me to say, 'Oh, I'm sorry; I didn't see you coming.' The event would be the same; my foot would be hurting just as much. But my feeling would now be embarrassment and my behavior would be apologetic.

"But then if the friend I was with told me, 'Don't be fooled by him. He's no more blind than you are. He just pretends to be blind in order to get people's attention,' my feeling would again be very different—I'd be angry—and I might like to hit the man or give him a piece of my mind. The event would be the same, but now I have a third set of feelings and a third kind of behavior in response to my feelings."

Marlene concluded: "Events don't cause feelings and feelings don't cause behavior. Something intervenes between the event and the feeling." Marlene then placed on the floor a fourth sheet of paper, positioning it from her audience's perspective below and between the papers with the words EVENT and FEELING. On this fourth page was written ATTITUDE.

"Attitudes," she said, "are decisions we've made about the way life is or the way it ought to be. These are not merely cognitive decisions; they have an emotional component as well. The events we experience are filtered through our attitudes. It is this filtering of events through our attitudes which generates the feelings we have."

Marlene explained more fully than I am now just what attitudes are and how events filter through them. Events do not directly cause feelings. Her foot felt the same in all three examples. The initial feeling of annoyance was generated as the event was filtered through the decision she had made prior to the incident—and quite independently of the particular incident—that people ought to be considerate enough of others not to walk into them or over them. The feeling of embarrassment was generated as the event was filtered through the decision that people ought to give way to someone who is blind. And the feeling of anger was generated as the event was filtered through the prior decision that people ought to act fairly in their dealings with others.

Marlene then turned her listeners' attention to the relationship between feelings and behavior. She pointed out that several behavior options were available to her. She could have chosen to speak harshly, to apologize or to hit the man. ''Behavior flows from decision,'' she said as she placed a fifth sheet of paper on the floor below and between those on which were written the words *FEELING* and *BEHAVIOR*. On this fifth page was the word *DECISION*.

She explained that behavior frequently flows so spontaneously from the way we feel that we don't know we are deciding or choosing our behavior. Our behavior is so spontaneous at times that it seems automatic. Frequently only in retrospect do we see that other options for behavior were available to us.

Not only in retrospect can we recognize the options for our behavior. We can also learn to slow down the spontaneous internal process enough to become aware that we decide on our behavior rather than experience an automatic reaction. In slowing down our internal psychic processes, we can learn to respond to events instead of merely reacting to them. We enable ourselves to decide freely about our behavior and become ''response-able'' for it.

I returned to Detroit the next day, anxious to share with Jerry the schema which seemed to represent accurately the interaction of those forces within us which we had been trying for months to understand.

Over the years since my evening with Marlene, Jerry and I have used the schema repeatedly to understand ourselves and to attempt to speak accurately about what we have come to understand. We've listened to other people speak and by means of this schema we've heard them—sometimes with an accuracy their speaking didn't have. We've developed the schema a bit since the drawing I attempted during our first conversation after the evening I spent with Marlene.

A couple of years later Marlene and I gave a workshop together. As we prepared for it I wanted us to present the schema to the participants as part of the workshop. It was initially her invention. Jerry and I had changed and enlarged it some since I had first heard Marlene present it. She asked me about the changes and developments. I told her about them. Her own thinking had enlarged and developed the schema too. Marlene suggested that the original idea had developed into two independent traditions flowing from the same source. Marlene is the source of the tradition Jerry and I have developed.

I write all this because my initial experience of the schema serves as the only way I know to introduce others to the "Sometimes Useful Tool." It doesn't seem right for me to introduce people to it without acknowledging that it would not exist except for my experience of that evening in Marlene's company.

For reasons I will elaborate in Chapter Four, Jerry and I changed what Marlene had labeled *EVENT* to

PERCEPTION and we came to understand attitude to be but one source within us through which we interpret what we perceive. We therefore changed *ATTITUDE* to *INTERPRETATION*. In its most basic format the "Sometimes Useful Tool" now looks like this:

Fig. 1

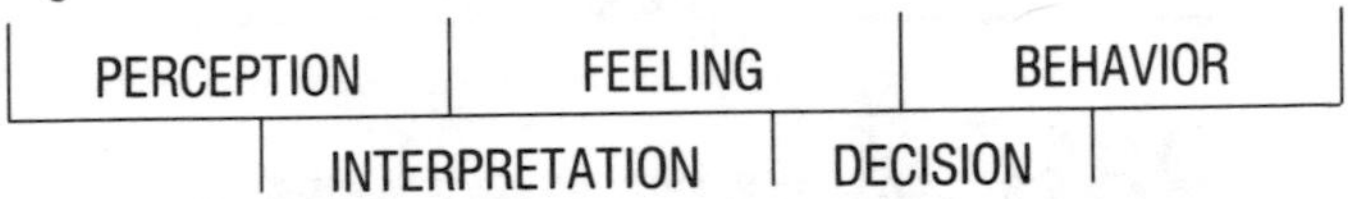

PERCEPTION	FEELING	BEHAVIOR
INTERPRETATION	DECISION	

Three

Self-Awareness and Self-Disclosure

We are all familiar with those scenes in which two people try simultaneously to relate the story of an incident they have recently experienced together. Usually one begins the narration and gets about as far into the story as mentioning that the event took place on Tuesday when the other says, ''No, it was on Monday, because, remember, we had tuna salad for lunch the day it happened, and we had tuna salad on Monday.'' The particular day of the week being unimportant to the narrator, the point is conceded, but usually in a way that indicates that the concession is made for the sake of getting on with the story, not because the correction is accepted as accurate.

The variant versions of each detail are narrated by the two people alternately from the debate about the day of the week in question right on through to the two versions of the usually less than dramatic conclusion ("You had to be there!"), after which each narrator summarizes the event with the moral of the story or the aspect of human life highlighted by the experience.

By recalling such scenes, I wish to highlight this aspect of human experience: Whenever we speak, regardless of the subject, we reveal ourselves. We may be narrating our memory of an incident, praising or defaming another's character, commenting on the world situation, suggesting plans for future group development, or wishing out loud for some desirable state of affairs. In doing so, we disclose to our hearers those aspects of which we were aware and which continue to have significance for us—our feelings, our opinions, our attitudes.

In our awareness of events, people and things we are limited by our perceptions, by the interpretation we give to what we perceive and by the feelings generated within us because we interpret our perception of the event or person or thing the way we do.

Our perceptions do have an objectivity about them; but our awareness of what we have perceived—and to some extent our awareness of our own internal states—is our awareness of them as we perceived and interpreted them, and not simply the way they are in themselves. I don't mean to begin a discussion on the mind's ability to know anything outside itself. I wish only to focus attention on the experience most people already have: incomplete, selective, inaccurate perception and subjective interpretation of what is perceived.

When I am unaware of the limited nature of my perception and the subjectivity of my interpretation, and when I focus my attention exclusively outside myself, I become a victim of the delusion my own lack of self-awareness has created. Convinced that my perception is accurate and complete and unaware that I have interpreted what I have perceived, I feel quite comfortable correcting others who have perceived and interpreted differently than I have and I am equally comfortable ignoring any correction someone else may offer me. I begin to live at least as much in "my own little world" as in "our world."

Human beings don't connect very well when they tell themselves that another's perception and interpretation of reality are wrong because they differ from their own. If connecting with others depends on identical perceptions and compatible interpretations of the world we share, the number of human beings with whom one thinks he or she can connect will be very limited. We have little incentive to connect with anyone who could be so wrong. To be so wrong a person would have to be very stupid, biased or brain-washed. Who would want to connect with someone like that?!

In order for people to connect through speaking to one another, their awareness of their perceptions and interpretations needs to become more reflective and reflexive. We need to recognize, in other words, that our awareness of our perceptions, interpretations and feelings is our self-awareness and that our disclosure of our perceptions and interpretations—as well as our feelings—is our self-disclosure.

The "Sometimes Useful Tool" can be helpful in doing the kind of reflection which will expand the parameters of my awareness of my perceptions to include the recognition that they are, in fact, my perceptions of reality; it can lead to the reflective thinking that will enlarge my awareness to include the recognition of the fact that I am interpreting what I perceive. When I convert my awareness to self-awareness, my disclosure becomes my self-disclosure instead of simply argument or agreement about the nature and shape of reality.

Perhaps the easiest way to use the "Sometimes Useful Tool" is to imagine it as an organizer of internal experience. I can think about what I know because of my perceptions, as well as what I think because of my interpretation of what I have perceived, as my *self*-awareness. It is therefore easier to think of my speaking about what I have perceived and interpreted as my *self*-disclosure.

Without the recognition that one perceives and interprets the world beyond one's inner experience in limited and subjective ways, it is unlikely that anyone will speak to others in any way other than to tell them the way the world is—in an effort, unconscious perhaps, to structure the other's inner world. That is manipulative and likely to establish a dominant/subservient relationship.

Every time we speak we tell our hearers something about ourselves. At times we intend to disclose ourselves. At other times we intend to tell our hearers about themselves or about some other person or an event or a thing. But in all cases we disclose ourselves.

When I speak about another person, event or thing, I may give my hearers information about that person, event or thing. But I disclose *my* perception and *my* interpretation of what I have perceived. My words don't give my hearers an experience of the subject. My speaking allows my hearers to experience me. Through my self-disclosure I allow another into my own inner psychic world and give him or her an experience of how I have arranged that inner world. If my interpretation of what I have perceived rings true with my hearer, he or she may be able and willing to interpret what he or she has perceived in a way similar to my interpretation. The hearer, through listening to my self-disclosure, is put in touch with his or her own experience and interpretation. In response to my interpretation, my hearer may re-interpret his or her perception of reality.

I have found it helpful to realize that I disclose myself when I speak and that I hear your self-disclosure when you speak. For instance, when I say that a meeting was beneficial and enlightening, I will be less likely to spend a lot of time arguing the relative merits of the event with someone who says the meeting was of no benefit at all if I recognize that I am disclosing my opinion of the meeting and the other person is disclosing his or her opinion. We would both be disclosing ourselves. A bystander who overheard our conversation would learn nothing about the meeting, but could learn something about both of us who were expressing our interpretation of an event we had experienced.

I have found it helpful to recognize not only that I disclose myself when I speak, but also what part of my inner psychic experience I disclose. I find it equally helpful to recognize what part of another's inner psychic experience he or she discloses in his or her speech.

Using the "Sometimes Useful Tool," I find it helpful to know whether I am disclosing my perception, my interpretation of what I have perceived or the feelings generated by the way I interpret what I perceive. If I know what I am disclosing, I am more able to choose the verbal expression which most properly discloses what I want. For instance, it is more appropriate to say, ''As I remember it, the meeting lasted for two hours without a break, and the two speakers gave talks about marketing and targeting the proper market (perception); I thought the first speaker was more clear than the second (interpretation); I got bored by the middle of the second speech (feeling)'' than to say, ''The meeting was long and boring.''

The ''Sometimes Useful Tool'' helps me sort out what I am aware of and what I might want to disclose of my awareness. It is helpful in choosing the appropriate expression of my inner awareness when I try to disclose it. It is also useful in organizing what I hear when others disclose themselves, perhaps in forms of expression not well suited for the type of disclosure they are making.

For instance, a person may tell me that a meeting was boring or exciting, beneficial or useless, too long or just about the right length. Using the ''Sometimes Useful Tool'' as a framework into which I fit what I hear of that disclosure, I can recognize that a meeting is neither boring nor exciting; the speaker feels bored or excited in response to his or her interpretation of what he or she experienced. I can recognize that a meeting is neither beneficial nor useless; the speaker judged or interpreted what he or she experienced as helpful or not for his or her own purposes. I can recognize that a meeting is not too long or just the right length; it lasted a definite amount of time which the person either did not perceive, has not remembered or has chosen not to report because the interpretation of the event has more significance for him or her.

Self-awareness, self-disclosure and hearing allow people who are strangers on the horizons of each others' lives to connect in a way that permits intimacy to arise between them. In hearing another's disclosure I still have no direct experience of what the other has perceived and interpreted in his or her unique way. I will not have had feelings generated in me because of the other's interpretation of what was perceived. But if I hear what the other discloses of himself or herself, I may be put in touch with my own similar experience.

I doubt if I ever really "know just what you mean" and "know just how you feel." When I hear you disclose yourself, I am put in touch with my own experience and my perception and interpretation of that experience. I know myself better because of having heard another's self-disclosure, and I know more surely that I am not the only one who has those kinds of experiences. I am not alone.

Four

Perceptions and Interpretations

A scene from the film ''Kim,'' which I saw when I was a child, has remained vivid for over thirty years. It returns to my consciousness many times and I've not yet been able to understand why it remains such a vivid memory.

In the scene Kim, a boy of perhaps 12, is beginning his instruction under the tutelage of the old teacher. Kim and a boy slightly younger than he, who has already been taught for some time by the master, are sitting with their teacher around the lamp-lit table. The master produces a small cloth-covered tray on which rest precious stones and gems, covered by the end of a peacock feather. The master removes the feather for a few seconds and replaces it. He asks Kim to name the items on the tray and their number. Kim begins haltingly to name the jewels but he is unsure of their exact nature and number.

The master then turns to the other lad and asks him to name the contents of the tray. He does so with a calm confidence that amazes Kim and pleases the master. Turning back to Kim the teacher explains that one needs to learn to use one's senses for what they can reveal. Kim's mistake was to use his mind on a task his eyes could do better alone. When seeing, one should concentrate on getting an accurate visual image; after the visual image is formed, one can use one's mind to name and interpret what has been seen.

Both the story and my attempt to narrate it over thirty years later illustrate the lesson the master was trying to teach Kim. What I perceive doesn't have meaning for me until I interpret it, but the two activities are distinct. The clarity of my perception may at times become obscured by my attempt to interpret what I have perceived.

I perceive with my senses. I see, hear, taste, smell or feel something. Feeling here refers to touch, not emotion. I include in my understanding of the sense of touch such things as the pain I feel in my body and those things I feel from the environment, such as heat and cold, wind or humidity. I become aware of things outside myself through my senses.

I disclose this awareness of mine through statements about what I saw, heard, smelled, tasted or touched. Those statements of what I have perceived can profitably be examined to determine whether they are reports of my perceptions or of my interpretations. I don't mean to imply that statements which disclose both one's perceptions and one's interpretation are necessarily inaccurate. But it can be helpful to distinguish the two mental operations.

Some examples may help to distinguish perception from interpretation.

"The man was happy" is a statement about the way someone else feels. Since no one perceives directly the emotion of another, it is a report of one's interpretation of what one has seen and heard of the man. In order to report a perception of the man, the person could say, "I saw him smiling. I heard him say that he was happy. I heard and saw him laugh." Neither statement is necessarily a more accurate description of the man than the other, nor is either statement more desireable or appropriate in describing the man. "The man was happy" is an interpretation the speaker made by assuming that smiling and laughter indicate happiness and that the speaker trusts the words of the man.

If later the man were to say that he had not been happy at the time, the one who reported it could still say, "I saw him smile. I heard him say he was happy. I heard and saw him laugh." Those perceptions remain accurate; that smiling and laughter indicate happiness is still a reasonable assumption; the decision to trust what people say may remain the attitude one chooses to espouse. But the interpretation of what one perceived seems now to have been inaccurate.

We perceive some things with our senses. Other things—feelings, attitudes, intentions, desires, assumptions, biases, prejudices of another—are never directly perceived. Attempts to tell ourselves that we have perceived any of these interior psychic phenomena in another are misguided. I can hear another's statement about these internal realities, and I can see behaviors of another that I interpret, perhaps correctly, as flowing from certain attitudes, feelings, assump-

31

tions, biases, prejudices and feelings in another. I don't, however, directly perceive these inner realities.

The language in which we speak, first to ourselves and then to others, can tell us whether our self-awareness or self-disclosure is of a perception or an interpretation. I express a perception in words that relate to the use of my senses. For instance, "I saw . . .", "I heard . . .", "I tasted . . .", "I smelled . . .", "I touched . . ." express my awareness of a perception. Other expressions convey the same meaning, such as "It felt . . . (cold)", "It was . . . (red)", "It sounded . . . (shrill)", "He was . . . (short)". Although not a direct report of what one saw, heard, tasted, smelled or touched, they convey perceptions. We perceive temperature, color, sound or size through the senses. Even such expressions as "He was shorter than she was," report what people perceive with their senses. Unless I indicate that I am aware of something through the use of my senses, my awareness and disclosure are not of a perception.

I can be aware of and disclose my attitudes, assumptions, biases, opinions, beliefs or preoccupations through which I interpret my perceptions. I can be aware of my intention in my behaving the way I did. Perhaps I am aware of my feelings toward what I have perceived and interpreted. But I am not aware of my *perceptions* unless I can speak about an event, a person, a thing, even my own behavior, in words that indicate that my awareness has come about by the function of one or more of my senses.

Even if a narration of an event does not include interpretation as well as perception, it is important to realize I didn't perceive the event being narrated. I hear the narration of another person's perception of the event. Possibly another witness to the same event would have perceived it differently. If I heard that other person narrate his or her version of the same event and it were different from the first version I heard, I would perhaps realize that no matter how vividly my own imagination constructed the event as I heard the first narration, I really didn't perceive it. I interpret any narration on the basis of an assumption that the other person is accurately or inaccurately reporting his or her perception.

The "Sometimes Useful Tool" is helpful in distinguishing perceptions from interpretations. We are so familiar with our inner psychic processes that we may think any further understanding of them is unnecessary. However, the number of conversations I take part in almost daily that are dissatisfying and even frustrating at times suggests I would connect better with others if we all understood better the difference between perception and interpretation.

I may engage in conversation with you and forget that in telling you anything about someone else or about an event or a thing—or even about my own behavior or yours—I am disclosing myself. I may fail to recognize whether I am disclosing my perception or my interpretation of what I have perceived. That will make connecting with you haphazard at best.

I'll use the "Sometimes Useful Tool" to examine and analyze my contribution to a recent conversation concerning eating at fast food places while traveling. First I'll give my part of the conversation without trying to sort out perception and interpretation. Before going on to my second account of the same incident, note the impression you get from my statements.

"It was a hot day and I was hungry, so I decided to stop to eat even though it was too late for lunch and too early for supper. I decided I'd drive until I got to Hardee's, because their chicken sandwich is the best, and I wanted a chicken sandwich; they are better for you than a hamburger.

"I had gotten my order of a chicken sandwich and fries and a cup of coffee and was sitting in a booth near the counter, facing the rest of the tables and booths in the place. A man came in. He had long stringy hair growing from the sides of his head. The top of his head was almost bald. The hair was oily, like he hadn't washed it in a long time.

"I didn't see what the man ordered, but he sat down right in the middle section of the restaurant, facing toward me. He was right out there in the open where everyone had to look at him. I watched him eat entirely too much—three hamburgers, a large order of fries and two milkshakes. And he ate in the most uncouth manner. He sat there in sight of everybody chewing his food with his mouth open, and pushing more food into his mouth before he had swallowed the last bite. It was disgusting to watch. I finally got up before I had finished my coffee and left the place because it was so disgusting to watch him that I couldn't even enjoy my coffee.

"I went down the road a couple more blocks and stopped at a Dairy Queen and got a Blizzard to eat with my coffee. So the guy really did me a favor by driving me out of Hardee's."

Taking that as my story of an incident, anyone who heard me could concentrate so much on the man in the story that he or she would miss entirely that I was also talking about myself in my disclosure of my awareness of that experience. If my hearer failed to distinguish my perceptions from my interpretations, feelings, decisions and behavior, he or she would be tempted to take the story as a report about someone else. If however the person were careful to distinguish my perceptions from my interpretations, the shape and import of the story could change. If my hearer realized that my narration was my self-disclosure, the effect of his or her hearing my story could be significantly different.

Labelled, the elements of the story look like this:

"It was a hot day (perception—touch) and I was hungry (perception—touch), so I decided to stop to eat (decision) even though it was too late for lunch and too early for supper (interpretation of the fact that it was 2:30 p.m.). I decided I'd drive until I got to Hardee's (decision), because their chicken sandwich is the best (interpretation—opinion), and I wanted a chicken sandwich (desire); that's better for you than a hamburger (interpretation—opinion).

"I had gotten my order of a chicken sandwich and fries and a cup of coffee and was sitting in a booth near the counter, facing the rest of the tables and booths in the place (perception of my own behavior). A man came in (perception—sight). He had long stringy hair growing from the sides of his head (perception—sight). The top of his head was almost bald (perception—sight). The hair was oily (perception—sight), like he hadn't washed it in a long time (interpretation—opinion or assumption).

"I didn't see what the man ordered, but he sat down right in the middle section of the restaurant, facing toward me (perception—sight). He was right out there in the open where everyone had to look at him (interpretation—assumption). I watched him eat entirely too much (interpretation—opinion)—two hamburgers, a large order of fries and two milkshakes (perception—sight). And he ate in the most uncouth manner (interpretation—opinion). He sat there in sight of everybody chewing his food with his mouth open, and pushing more food into his mouth before he had swallowed the last bite (perception—sight). It was disgusting to watch (feeling expressed indirectly, in place of "I was disgusted"). I finally got up before I had finished my coffee and left the place (perception of my own behavior) because it was so disgusting to watch him that I couldn't (decision—although responsibility for it is denied) even enjoy my coffee (feeling).

"I went down the road a couple more blocks and stopped at a Dairy Queen and got a Blizzard to eat with my coffee (perception of my own behavior). So the guy really did me a favor (interpretation—opinion) by driving me out of Hardee's (decision—although responsibility for it is denied)."

In the following chapter I will look more closely at the ways we interpret what we perceive. For now, note that in this narration, I disclose myself. True, you can gain some information about the man I talked about. But you still have no experience of him. You take my word for the fact that he looked and acted as I said he did. You experience my disclosure of my perceptions. You also heard me disclose how I felt, what I decided, how I behaved and how I interpreted what I perceived. You experienced me in this narration, because it is my self-disclosure of my self-awareness.

Using the "Sometimes Useful Tool," what you learned about me in my narration can be charted as in Fig. 2 below.

This is perhaps a very clinical way to look at the narration of one man's perception of an incident. And the incident in question probably doesn't need that close an analysis. But many conversations about people, events and things are not nearly so innocuous. In these more significant conversations, failure to recognize that all disclosure is self-disclosure, and failure to recognize the difference between a disclosure of one's perceptions and a disclosure of one's interpretation can lead to a great many misunderstandings where there could have been a connection made between two human beings.

The greater failure, though, is to be unaware that within oneself there are perceptions and interpretations. This lack of awareness can cause distortions in one's disclosure which make it virtually impossible for him or her to connect with any but a very few human beings—those who are equally unaware of the distinction of perception and interpretation and who happen to interpret the world in the same way.

37

Fig. 2

PERCEPTIONS	FEELINGS	BEHAVIORS
hot day; hungry; man enters; stringy hair; almost bald; oily hair; man sat; man ate hamburgers, large order of fries, two milkshakes; man chewed with mouth open; added food to mouth before swallowing previous bite	disgust; not enjoying	drove until I reached Hardee's; ordered chicken sandwich, fries and coffee; sat down; watched man; left restaurant; drove to Dairy Queen; ordered Blizzard

INTERPRETATIONS	DECISIONS
too late for lunch, too early for supper; Hardee's is the best chicken sandwich; chicken sandwiches are better for you than hamburgers; oily hair is not washed; man ate too much; manner of eating was uncouth; man did me a favor	to stop to eat; to drive to Hardee's; not to finish coffee; to leave Hardee's; to stop at Dairy Queen; to order a Blizzard

How We Interpret

The president of the United States had just finished a news conference. The newscasters' and commentators' faces immediately filled the television screen, speaking to their audiences and with each other in a general re-hash of what the president had said. Each one interpreted this or that part of the speech in the light of something which he or she deemed important. In the living room viewers listened to the news conference and the commentaries offered by the media personalities. Each critiqued what the commentators said, pointing out the biases they thought they recognized in the comments. None of the viewers was in agreement with any of the others on just what the news conference and the subsequent commentaries had given them by way of accurate information. Some doubted the veracity of the president's words; others disputed the interpretation given by the reporters.

Nowhere more than in such a news conference does it become evident that people know they are dealing with the interpretations of what is perceived and presented; it is equally obvious that people deal with the matter of interpretations with ease. No one seems ready to accept as fact what either the political leader or the commentators said. They seem ready to examine what they have heard and to try to separate the perceptions from the interpretations.

I don't know what that says about political leaders and their speaking to their public. I think it suggests that people are equipped to understand the role interpretation plays in our internal experience of reality and in our speaking to one another about our experience. I also think it indicates that people are prepared to examine within themselves the possibility that they too interpret what they perceive.

The "Sometimes Useful Tool" includes the category of "Interpretation." I have found it helpful to recognize what general means we use for interpreting what we perceive. I doubt I have constructed an exhaustive list, but my list may provide some incentive for others to examine what they find within themselves.

It seems to me less important to label a particular type of interpretation than to recognize that I am interpreting. I include in my list the following general categories: opinions, assumptions, attitudes, biases, preoccupations and beliefs.

The interpretation I do when I think about what I perceive is *opinion*. Opinions are judgments I make about the nature or the qualities of another person, an event or a thing. Opinions can be detached, in the sense that I simply think something about a perception and judge what I am thinking to be accurate in the light of my experience and knowledge. A disclosure of an opinion indicates that I am the one thinking and what I am thinking.

The following are opinions:

"He's an honest man."

"She told the truth."

"The apples are not ripe."

"It's going to rain."

"They will arrive before noon."

"The kids are happy."

With each of these expressions the danger is that both the speaker and the hearer could fail to recognize that I think these thoughts. They could all be mistaken for a statement of what one has perceived and not a statement about the way one has interpreted that perception by making a judgment. A more accurate disclosure of the opinions might be the following:

"I think he's an honest man."

"In my opinion she told the truth."

"The apples don't seem ripe to me."

"I think it's going to rain."

"I expect them to arrive before noon."

"The kids seem happy to me."

When we say to another, "He's an honest man," or "She told the truth," or "They'll be here by noon," we may forget that we are disclosing something about ourselves. We often think we are informing our hearers about the other people and expect our hearers to take what we say as an accurate perception. We can be insulted if our hearers choose to reject our opinions as not helpful in formulating their own. We can also feel imposed upon by others who seem to forget they are disclosing something about themselves and seem to demand that we accept their statement of opinion as a perception of reality.

I think (opinion) we would all do well to recognize that our opinions are interpretations we give to what we have perceived by the judgments we make about our perceptions. We should further recognize that the statement of our opinions is a disclosure of ourselves and not merely the giving of information about the way things are.

Assumption is the interpretation I give to what I perceive on the basis of what I know to be true of myself or on the basis of my previous experience of another person, event or thing. Assumption takes for granted something that even I don't tell myself I have perceived.

Assumptions are frequently expressed as generalizations, either of the kind which suggest that "everybody does . . ." or the kind which suggest that "you/he/she/they always . . ." They are rarely expressed in statements which begin "I assume . . ." Assumptions are harder to recognize in a conversation than opinions.

I would like to take that last sentence and use it as an example of what I mean. "Assumptions are harder to recognize than opinions," is my opinion. I know I have a more difficult time recognizing in the speech patterns of others their expression of assumptions, and I take for granted that others have the same difficulty I have. I interpret what I perceive of others on the basis of what is true of me.

When I tell myself or another, "I know what you mean," or "I know how you feel," I interpret what I have come to know of another's experience on the basis of what I know to be true of myself. A much more accurate self-disclosure would be, "When I hear you say that, I am put in touch with my own feelings in a situation which I think was similar."

Sometimes I am inclined to say to another, "You always . . ." I take that to be an indication that I am interpreting the other's behavior on the basis of an assumption. A more accurate statement of that assumption would be, "I have come to expect of you that . . ." Such a statement would indicate that I am interpreting what I perceive of your behavior on the basis of past experience. It would more clearly be a disclosure of myself.

Often we express the assumptions by which we interpret another's behavior so indirectly that it is difficult to recognize them. For instance, while camping last summer I heard a man say to his son as the son emerged from his tent at 10 a.m., "Are you sick?" My assumption was that the father assumed that emerging from the tent late indicated some illness on the part of his son.

I heard (perception) a man say, "Are you sick?" to a younger man whom I saw (perception) coming out of a tent at 10 a.m. On the basis of what might prompt me to ask such a question, I assumed (interpretation) that the father was making the inquiry on the assumption that he would not stay in bed until 10 a.m. unless he were ill. So I assumed the father was making the assumption I would make. This may or may not have been perfectly accurate.

An *attitude* is a decision I have made about the way a part or all of life is or ought to be. That decision is made and espoused consciously or unconsciously prior to any perception or interpretation. Prejudices of all kinds are attitudes. I may be introduced to a man who is a lawyer, and before I see or hear anything of him, I may have decided that he is an extremely honest man. Or I may have decided that he is out to get all he can from others.

Like opinions and assumptions, attitudes are cognitive; that is, they have to do with what I think. Attitudes are also emotional, that is, based on what I feel. Opinions can change when we obtain and accept further information. Assumptions can change when I am confronted with evidence that my interpretations are based on criteria that do not fit the particular case. For example, the father of the son in the previous story may have told me that the rest of the family had gotten sick during the night and he was wondering about his son's health.

Attitudes change only with more information and much more experience, because they are decisions I have made about life itself or some part of life.

For instance, if I have decided that life is unfair, I won't easily change that attitude just because I hear of someone being treated fairly. I can receive and accept the cognitive evidence, but that does not change the emotional component of my decision.

I do not need a great deal of evidence to induce me to espouse a certain attitude. One bad experience with a lawyer can prejudice me against all lawyers, not because of the overwhelming cognitive evidence I have at my disposal, but because of the emotional component of that decision. The emotional component will induce me to attend only to such evidence as supports my already espoused attitude.

I have come to think that attitudes are not easily recognized by the person who espouses them. Others are liable to recognize an attitude in me before I do. If, for instance, in my conversations with others, I am always contributing the "Yes, but . . ." comment when something or someone is being spoken of positively, those who hear me do this often enough may recognize in me a pessimistic or otherwise negative attitude toward life long before I see it myself. If I repeatedly report on the incompetence of my superiors or my peers, even when my situation brings me into contact with different superiors and a different group of peers, those who hear me could probably recognize in me an attitude of inferiority for which I compensate by my criticism of others.

Attitudes are not easily changed. But if I can begin to recognize what my attitudes are, I can more easily espouse consciously the ones I approve and be less swayed by the ones I don't approve as I interpret what I perceive of others.

Biases may be one kind of attitude. I distinguish them from other attitudes, however, in that they seem to be interpretations I give to things, events or persons in comparison to others. I can be biased for or against a person, event or thing on the basis of almost incidental qualities in them. I can be biased in favor of a color, for instance, or a combination of colors. Something totally red may repel me, while something red, white and blue may attract me.

I can be biased in favor of people with blond hair and against people with brown hair. I can be biased in favor of people who have a particular characteristic of body or outlook and against people who don't have that characteristic. In any case, my interpretation is influenced, almost predetermined, before I perceive anything beyond the particular characteristic about which I am biased. I might get a glimpse of my biases if

I made two lists of contrasting people, events or things by completing the sentence, "I prefer _____ to _____ ."

Preoccupations are ways I interpret what I perceive on the basis of what I hope for, what I fear or what I deem important. If I fear not being trusted by others, I will likely interpret other people's behavior as being mistrusting regardless of whether or not they actually trust me. It may seem to others that I will find ways of interpreting a given interaction with another person as the other's lack of trust in me. I may hope people will like what I have just said or done. If that is my preoccupation, I'll take almost anything someone says to me as a sign that they liked my performance. One favorable comment from one person may convince me that everybody liked what I did. If I fear not being liked, on the other hand, one negative comment may convince me that everyone disliked my actions or words.

As I work on this manuscript, I am preoccupied with the importance of communication in human life. I engage in conversations with others or even overhear conversations between two people, and pay less attention to the topic of the conversations than to the manner in which they communicate.

I have included *beliefs* as a means of interpreting what I perceive, and by this I mean religious faith. Religious faith certainly gives one opinions, assumptions, attitudes, biases and preoccupations. Beyond those, however, religious faith is the sense one has that "I know I am known by the Other." This sense includes knowing that the Other knows one's attitudes, assumptions, preoccupations and biases. The sense of faith turns over to the Other the judgment on the correctness of all the interpretation one gives to life and all the interpretation others give to the believer's life. It accepts that one's interpretation is fallible no matter how satisfyingly articulated and firmly held.

Faith is the most difficult of all interpretations to articulate. Almost all attempts to articulate one's faith find expression in a theological statement. All theological statements are opinions. Only on rare occasions does one get a glimpse of his or her own faith; even more rarely does one get a glimpse of another's faith. These glimpses are never contained in a statement. Faith is experienced in oneself and glimpsed in another almost as superstition while at the same time being recognized as other than superstition. Faith is the interpretation of what is perceived as ineffable, not speakable and yet seeking to be spoken.

I find it helpful to distinguish these various ways of interpreting what one perceives for two reasons. First, I have become convinced (opinion and preoccupation) that it is important to distinguish my interpretation from my perception. I have been helped in this by looking at statements I make and then analyzing them to see if they are my opinions, assumptions, attitudes, biases, preoccupations or faith. Facility in recognizing the means by which I interpret what I perceive, both in my self-awareness and my self-disclosure and in listening to what others say, has grown in me because I have used the "Sometimes Useful Tool."

The second reason is this: In most cases I need to recognize that other people have a limited responsibility for my interpretation of their words and actions. Conversely, I have a limited responsibility for how others interpret what they perceive of me. When the meaning of some action is rather strongly determined by human convention, however, and I act for purposes other than those suggested by human convention, I have a greater responsibility to disclose my intention or the meaning I give to my performing of the action. I have a limited responsibility to help others avoid misinterpreting my actions. My failure to give that help can reasonably be construed by others as my wanting to deceive or manipulate them.

_____ Six _____

Feelings

The way we interpret what we perceive generates feelings in us. Our perception does not generate the feeling, our interpretation does.

In the example Marlene used, the same event—a man stepping on her foot—generated three different feelings, depending on how she interpreted the event. First, she was annoyed because she interpreted the man's action as inconsiderate. When she thought the man was blind, she was embarrassed because she interpreted the cause of the event as her lack of awareness of one who was handicapped. When she thought the man was just pretending to be blind, she was angry because she interpreted the man's actions as unfair.

How we feel is usually one of the first things that tries to enter our consciousness when we meet a person, encounter a situation or come into contact with an object. Our feelings could be that part of our internal experience most accessible to us; but frequently they are the last part of our internal experience to be acknowledged. I wonder if we suppress full consciousness of our feelings because we wouldn't know what to do with them if we were to acknowledge them.

Disclosure of feelings is frequently the most difficult for people to make. Attempts to disclose feelings often end up in a disclosure of opinion or perception. "That was a great hit," a father may tell his little league son, when he was most immediately in touch with his feeling of pride over what he had just seen his offspring do. "You're a great mother," may be the verbal substitute for an articulation of the emotion of gratitude a son or daughter feels in response to a kindness done by the mother. "You're too kind," finds its way to the lips of people who are feeling appreciation for what another has done.

The list of examples in which someone substitutes a statement of an opinion, however positive, for a disclosure of emotion could fill this chapter and many more. I heard it said once, and it appears to be true, that there is a continuum of difficulty with which emotions are reported. The least difficult to report are feelings I've had about somebody else in the past: "I was angry with him all last school year." Somewhat more difficult is the report of feelings I currently have about someone else: "I don't like her." More difficult still is the disclosure of feelings I had in the past about you: "I used to get so annoyed at you when we were in college." And the most difficult of all is the disclosure of emotions I am having about you now: "I like you."

I suspect people frequently ignore or deny their feelings even in their own self-awareness because they are reluctant to disclose them. If I don't know what to do with my feelings—how to report them—why bother paying attention to them? This deprives us of a great deal of potentially valuable information. My feelings tell me what something means to me. I have opinions about what something means; but my feelings alert me to what something means to me. Often in an attempt to "be objective," people ignore or deny their feelings, preferring to try to understand and express what a situation means "objectively" rather than to acknowledge what a situation means to them personally.

Ignoring or denying our feelings because they can be difficult to deal with is a bit like deciding that it is entirely unnecessary to have things be different colors. Depriving ourselves of recognition of colors can be costly, as for instance in traffic signs and lights. Depriving ourselves of the data our feelings give us can be just as costly.

I have feelings whether I acknowledge and own them or not. Those feelings affect my behavior even when I keep myself unaware of them. I might not say, for instance, that I'm angry; but I may speak angrily, walk with an angry gait, scowl while listening to someone or be curt with people with whom I'm usually friendly. If asked by someone whether I'm angry, I may say, "No, I'm not angry. What makes you think I am?" The other person may point out the behavior I have been exhibiting and say, "Well, you talk mad."

My behavior has consequences. If I don't know how my feelings affect my behavior, I will frequently be unaware of my behavior too. I can suffer the consequences of my own behavior, and remain firmly convinced that my suffering is the result of other people's behavior, not my own. For instance, if I am angry and that anger is finding expression in my speaking, my facial expression, my walk and my being short with people, others are liable to begin to avoid me. If I don't see how my behavior could induce people to avoid me, I might begin to think they are angry with me. I might begin to consider myself a victim of other people's anger when, in fact, I am the victim of the consequences of my own behavior, because I choose to ignore or deny my own anger.

Besides finding an outlet in my behavior, my feelings can come out in physiological symptoms. When people's emotional lives are on even keel and up-beat, their physical health seems to be better. When people are embarrassed, they blush, an amazing physiological response to an emotional state. An ulcer caused by stress is another example of physiological symptoms generated by feelings.

Another way my feelings find a way out of me without my adverting to them directly occurs when I shift the focus of my attention from my feelings to some characteristic of a person, event or object about which I am having those feelings. My statement, first to myself and then to others, is a judgment about someone or something other than myself. "You're so stupid," indirectly expresses my frustration at your failure to understand what I'm trying to teach you. "The food was delicious," is a judgment about food, an indirect expression of "I liked the meal."

In these indirect expressions of feelings I move back one step in the "Sometimes Useful Tool" and focus my attention on my opinion or assumption about a person, event or thing. I tell myself what something means instead of telling myself what something means to me.

I have thought at times that many of us are so in

touch with our interpretations that we are not in touch with our perceptions or our feelings. We would rather tell ourselves and others what something means than state what we actually saw, heard, smelled, touched or tasted. We also prefer an interpretation to a disclosure of what we feel as a result of the way we interpret our perceptions.

When one speaks to oneself and to others using indirect expressions of one's feelings, it is equivalent to ignoring or denying the feelings in favor of focusing attention on someone or something outside of oneself. Speaking in these forms may provide a disclosure of one's opinions about other people or things, but it does not disclose one's feelings except obliquely.

The only constructive thing one can do with one's feelings is to be aware of them, to own them and to disclose them by means of a direct report. Being careful about the way I speak to myself and to others about my feelings helps me develop my own awareness of my feelings.

A direct report of feelings involves two elements: an indication that I am the one having the feeling, and an indication of the feeling I am having. The indication of the feeling I am having can be done in three ways:

1) I say, "I feel . . . " or "I am . . . " and follow this with a label ("angry"); the more simple "I like . . ." also fits in here.
2) I say, "I feel like . . ." and use a metaphor ("a fifth wheel" or "a motherless child").
3) I say, "I feel like . . . " and follow this with a description of an action I would like to perform ("giving you a big hug" or "shaking that man right out of his socks").

One kind of indirect expression that disguises itself as a direct report of feeling goes like this: "I feel that you are out to get me." "I feel that this meeting is too long." In both of these examples, the word *feel* is used, but what follows is a judgment about "you" or about "this meeting."

Here are some further examples.

"I feel like crying" (direct report: "I feel like . . . " and description of an action I would like to perform).

"Ralph is so disgusting" (indirect expression: a judgment about Ralph).

"Oh, how lovely!" (indirect expression: a judgment about something).

"I didn't like the meal" (direct report: "I like . . .").

"That meal was lousy" (indirect expression; a judgment about the meal).

"I feel like crawling into a hole and pulling it in after me" (direct report: "I feel like . . ." and a description of the action I'd like to perform).

"I felt that the movie was too long" (indirect expression; a judgment about the length of the movie).

"I'm angry" (direct report: "I am . . ." followed by a label).

"How can you be so stupid?!" (indirect expression: a judgment about another's intelligence expressed in the form of a question).

"I was disgusted with the way he ate his food" (direct report: "I feel . . ." followed by a label, with the object of the feeling specified).

"I felt good about the workshop" (direct report: "I felt . . ." followed by a label; with the object of the feeling specified).

"I felt that the music was too loud" (indirect expression: a judgment about the volume of the music).

"I like you" (direct report: "I like . . .").

Taking the time to recognize that my emotional circuitry is charged and to articulate that charge can be a helpful way to allow my feelings to enter my self-awareness. It may take some practice at first. The "Sometimes Useful Tool" can be used to practice identifying my feelings, what my feelings are about, and how I am interpreting what I have perceived.

I have frequently taken the time to draw the outline of the "Sometimes Useful Tool" and to sit with it to try to sort out my feelings and my interpretation of what I have perceived. In its simplest form the process looks like this:

Fig. 3

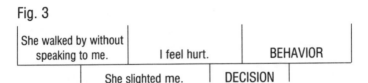

She walked by without speaking to me.	I feel hurt.	BEHAVIOR
	She slighted me.	DECISION

I may begin with the recognition that I have some feeling charging through my emotional circuits. At first, I may not be able to name it, but I know it is there. I can look to see what has happened—what I perceived—that may have generated some feeling. Then I may recognize how I am interpreting what I perceived. Finally, the emotion I am experiencing may come into focus for me; I may be able to name it or otherwise describe my emotional state to myself.

This is the simplest possible scenario. My own internal workings are seldom so simple. I rarely have one emotion at a time. They usually come in bunches, because I simultaneously interpret the same perception in a variety of ways. Let's follow the example through into a bit more complicated scenario.

Someone I know walks by me without acknowledging my presence. I begin to get some feelings: "I'm hurt, because I interpret her actions as a slight to me. I'm worried, because I interpret her actions to mean our friendship is coming to an end. I'm angry with her, because I think what she did was unfair. I'm puzzled, because I don't know how to interpret her actions. I feel guilty, because I interpret her actions as some kind of a response to something I must have done wrong." There may be more, but let's settle for these.

Fig. 4

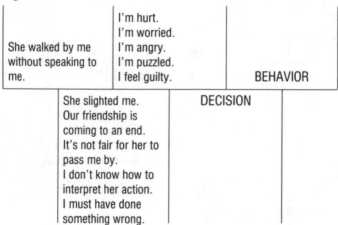

If that's not complicated enough, a current event can recall my perception of other events, and I recall my interpretation of those and another set of contradictory emotions overwhelms me. (See Fig. 5.)

With all this going on inside, there is little wonder

Fig. 5

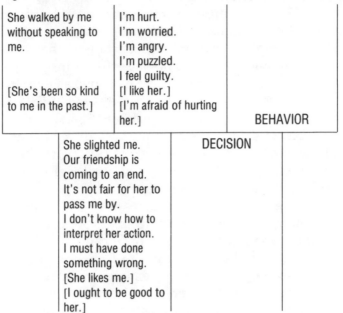

| She walked by me without speaking to me.

[She's been so kind to me in the past.] | I'm hurt.
I'm worried.
I'm angry.
I'm puzzled.
I feel guilty.
[I like her.]
[I'm afraid of hurting her.] | BEHAVIOR |
| | She slighted me.
Our friendship is coming to an end.
It's not fair for her to pass me by.
I don't know how to interpret her action.
I must have done something wrong.
[She likes me.]
[I ought to be good to her.] | DECISION |

that I would be hard pressed to say to myself or to someone else what I was feeling. Even if one does not take the time to write out the mental processes, the "Sometimes Useful Tool" can at least alert us to the large amount of information currently going through our system.

It seems almost unfair to add more complication to this matter, but I must. Another reason why we do not allow ourselves to become aware of our feelings and why we don't readily disclose them is that we have feelings about our feelings.

We perceive our feelings instead of just experiencing them. What we feel now becomes the data of our perception. Most of us learned very young that we ought to feel a certain way about the feelings we have! I believe that is an entirely unnecessary bit of learning with great disadvantages; but it happens.

For example, I may have been taught that it is wrong to be angry. Perhaps no one actually instructed me in that bit of information, but I have picked it up by implication. When I was angry, perhaps my initial expression was through unacceptable behavior. I may have been corrected or even punished for my behavior. I may not have had teachers skilled enough to help me understand that my anger was all right even though my behavior was wrong.

However it came about, it seems obvious we have a lot of feelings about a lot of our feelings. So, one more time, the "Sometimes Useful Tool" can help clarify what's going on. Let's just say I'm feeling angry because I interpret as unfair my seeing her walk by without speaking to me. Whether or not I focus on my anger in my self-awareness, I may interpret my anger as wrong or unworthy, and as a result I may feel guilty.

Using the "Sometimes Useful Tool," my internal state may be visualized this way:

Fig. 6

I feel angry.	I feel guilty.	BEHAVIOR
	Feeling angry is wrong.	DECISION

But of course, this feeling I have about one of the feelings generated by my interpretation of an event is simultaneous with all the feelings generated by all my interpretations of the event and all the feelings generated by all the interpretations of the memories the

Fig. 7

She walked by me without speaking to me.	I'm hurt. I'm worried. I'm angry. I'm puzzled. I feel guilty.	
[She's been so kind to me in the past.]	[I like her.] [I'm afraid of hurting her.]	
(I feel angry.)	(I feel guilty.)	BEHAVIOR
	She slighted me. Our friendship is coming to an end. It's not fair for her to pass me by. I don't know how to interpret her action. I must have done something wrong. [She likes me.] [I ought to be good to her.] (It's wrong to be angry.)	DECISION

event brings back to me. So, in the example we've been using, it would look like Fig. 7.

It's no wonder that to the question, ''How are you?'' people answer a simple ''Fine!'' And it's understandable that it can be difficult to answer the question, ''What are you feeling?'' even when one asks it only of oneself.

It has become part of popular conceptualization that one cannot change one's feelings and that there is no morality to feelings. I assent to those assertions. But I nuance them a bit more than I usually hear others doing.

I cannot change feelings directly by any willful demand I might make on myself to feel differently. However, if feelings result from the way I interpret my perceptions through my attitudes, assumptions and opinions, I do have some indirect control over my feelings. I am responsible for my interpretation of my perceptions, and at times I may have a moral obligation to change my interpretations.

For instance, I may not be able to change my feeling of fear at the sight of a person of another race or at the sound of a language other than my own being spoken. But if my fear is generated because of a prejudiced attitude toward other races or cultures, I can change the feeling by changing the prejudice. I can't make the change immediately, but I can deliberately attempt to gain experience which will modify the emotional component of my prejudiced attitude. I have a moral obligation to do so.

Or again, if my interpretation of one of my own actions leads to a feeling of discomfort, I can change the feeling by changing the interpretation. If I judge the action in a given instance to be morally good or neutral, I can freely choose to perform the action. The emotional component of my attitude can be addressed almost exclusively by performance of the action I judge to be good but about which I feel uncomfortable. Probably no moral obligation compels me to address my discomfort by performing the action, however.

Or again, if I dislike a person because I interpret his or her actions on the basis of an assumption that the action means to the other what it would mean if I did it, I can confront that assumption and my feeling can change. I may have some moral obligation to refrain from judging the actions of another on the basis of my own intention if I performed the action.

I don't suppose it is important to be able to ascertain all the perceptions, interpretations and feelings that might be going on inside of me at one time. I do suggest that the "Sometimes Useful Tool" is helpful in organizing my internal experiences in a way that allows me to recognize and reflect on them with some degree of sophistication, and so increase my self-awareness.

The "Sometimes Useful Tool" is helpful in my attempts at self-disclosure too. If I can with some degree of accuracy distinguish my perceptions from my interpretations and these from my feelings, I can choose words that will more accurately convey my inner experience, and I can make it clear to those who hear me that it is my inner experience I disclose. My accurate self-disclosure helps me connect with other human beings in ways other than gossip or the mutual exchange of ignorance or prejudice.

I also find the "Sometimes Useful Tool" helpful for hearing what others disclose of themselves. I will be less likely to accept as fact their description of people and things and their narration of events, because I will recognize that they disclose their perceptions. I may be less naively certain that I understand reality as a result of hearing them. I will recognize that primarily people disclose themselves in their narrations and descriptions. I will, however, be more attentive to the person to whom I am listening, and perhaps I will feel more free to disclose my perceptions and interpretations when I know them to be different from what I have heard. That may allow me to connect more fully with the person who discloses them to me.

What I perceive allows me to make my way around the real world without stumbling over everything. Through my interpretations I make sense out of the real world. My feelings tell me what things mean to me. The fact that things and people exist and that events happen doesn't move me to act; nor does the fact that these have meaning. What moves me to action is that things have meaning for me. My feelings induce me to choose behavior in an attempt to alter the shape of the world for better or worse.

Seven

The Third Party Ploy

I want to say one more thing about feelings. I consider it so important that I've decided to use a special chapter. It concerns not one's awareness of one's own feelings, but the awareness of the feelings other people have disclosed.

I learned this viewpoint over 20 years ago from friends who had heard Dr. Virgil Brown enunciate his "Techniques for Failure." The first of Dr. Brown's Techniques for Failure is what I have come to call the "Third Party Ploy" in dealing with other people's feelings. After testing out this technique for over 20 years, I know the truth of what my friends reported that Dr. Brown said.

The Third Party Ploy goes like this:

Our mutual friend tells me he is angry about something you have done. In an effort to bring the two of you closer together or to prompt you to take some action which will assuage our mutual friend's anger, I tell you he is angry with you.

No matter how fervently I hope to bring the two of you closer together by telling you about our mutual friend's feelings toward you, and no matter how carefully I couch my statements to you, I have just engaged in a technique bound to fail absolutely every time I use it.

I have recognized three versions of this destructive technique in relationships: the "Third Party Mistake," the "Claim of Shared Feelings" and the "Tobit Treatment."

The Third Party Ploy in any of its forms will destroy or impede connectedness among human beings. I emphasize the importance of understanding this technique because I would like to convince you never to allow yourself for any reason to become the third party reporting one person's feelings to the other.

In its simplest form the Third Party Ploy is the "Third Party Mistake." It occurs when Party Three discloses to Party Two what Party Three has learned from Party One about the feelings Party One has for the Party Two.

At times to be able to tell another person how one feels about yet another person is a source of great relief or release. At other times it is simply a disclosure one person makes to another in the course of a conversation. "I feel hurt because Jan slighted me," is a simple example. Or "I'm disappointed in my son Jerry's performance in school." "I'm embarrassed by Don's behavior." "I'm angry with Jean." There's no problem with that simple disclosure.

But if I am the one to whom these disclosures were made, I must never convey the speaker's feelings to the other person. It would be a mistake, no matter what my hope or intention, for me to say to Jan, "Mary is hurt because she thinks you slighted her." It would be a mistake for me to say to Jerry, "You know, your dad is disappointed in you because of your low grades." It would be a mistake for me to say to Don, "Your wife is embarrassed by your behavior." It would be a mistake for me to say to Jean, "Dennis is angry with you."

Let me press my point even further. It would be a mistake for me to make those kinds of statements even if my sole purpose in doing so was to help heal what I see as a deteriorating relationship, and even if I couch my report of the other person's feelings in all kinds of minimizing language. It will affect Jan's and Mary's relationship just as negatively whether I simply say, "Mary is hurt because she thinks you slighted her," or I launch into a speech filled with advice and good intentions: "I have something I want to tell you for your own good. I think you could improve your relationship with Mary if you would go out of your way to greet her next time you happen to see her. I know how much you like Mary. It might be good if you would show her that by just the little things, like greeting her, as well as by the larger things which you do so well. *Mary told me that she's been hurt just a bit by your not greeting her when you just happen to pass her by.* I'm sure it's not much of a hurt, but I know how much she means to you. It could help a lot of you'd pay special attention to her for awhile."

That whole speech would be just fine if it didn't contain the one sentence which says so clearly, "Mary has been talking to me about her feelings toward you."

If I would convey to any of the people mentioned above— Jan, Jerry, Don or Jean—the feelings of the one who confided in me, I would build a wall between them. Whatever I may intend, I would let the person know that the other is talking to me (and perhaps to others) about him or her. Since I am not telling the person my own feelings, the person cannot respond to my disclosure in any constructive way. Speaking with me will do nothing to address the feelings I have reported, because those feelings are not my own.

My own feelings tell me what something means to me. If I tell you my feelings about you, I'm telling you what you or your actions mean to me. You can respond to that significant information I have given you about myself. Whether or not you ever heard of the "Sometimes Useful Tool," you will know that I have perceived something about you and that I have interpreted it in a way which has meaning for me. You can then check out what I have perceived and how I have interpreted it.

If I tell you about another's feelings toward you, however, I am giving you significant information to which you can hardly make an adequate response. I cannot tell you exactly what the other person perceived about you; nor can I tell you exactly what significance that perception had for the other. It would do you very little good to try to explain to me what you think is needed in order to modify the other person's perception or explain to me your intention in order to modify the other person's interpretation of what he or she perceived.

If I tell you another person's feelings about you, I have burdened you with information about which you can do nothing. You would undoubtedly like the opportunity to speak to the one who has feelings about you and have him or her speak back to you. But you have only me, and you know that the other person chose to speak to me instead of to you. Another brick is put into place in the wall that separates the two of you; and I put it in place by engaging in the "Third Party Mistake."

Positive feelings reported by a third party may not be as devastating to hear as negative feelings, but they create the same problems for the one who hears the report from a third party.

The second version of the Third Party Ploy is the "Claim of Shared Feeling." I think people can agree on their perception and interpretation of something. But the feelings generated by the shared perception and interpretation are still very individual and entirely too nuanced to be reported as though they made up some sort of group resolution. What something means can be expressed in a shared statement of perception and interpretation; but what something means to me is not so readily shared.

When we use the "Claim of Shared Feeling," we make a statement about feelings that begins with "We feel . . ." and the "we" is specified. Let me use an example that could easily take place in my current situation as a member of a high school staff.

Let's say I have been deputed by the faculty to have a heart-to-heart talk with the members of the senior class. In the course of a good discussion about what has been happening in the school, I may tell the seniors what the faculty members collectively and cumulatively have perceived of the seniors' behavior. I may even tell them the faculty has reached some consensus on an interpretation of their perceptions. "We have seen you show up late for classes; we have heard you speak on occasion with some disrespect for some faculty members. We have seen you conspicuously absent from all school activities except those which are mandatory. We have begun to think that you have lost interest in the school and that you are behaving in ways designed to resist the school's program." So far, so good.

But if I attempt to report a shared feeling of the faculty, I have overstepped my bounds; I have said something which will build walls, not bridges. "We feel quite apprehensive about having you continue in the school. In fact, some of us can't wait for you to graduate. We're angry with you and disappointed in you. We're hurt by your behavior and suspicious of your intentions."

If I were to make such a claim of shared feelings among the faculty members, I would undoubtedly be remembering feelings I heard expressed by individual faculty members. Each statement I made would be true of someone.

In hearing my claim that the specified "we"—the faculty—share a certain feeling, the individual members of the senior class would undoubtedly think of individual members of the faculty. An individual senior boy might well wonder why the faculty member to whom he had spoken just ten minutes prior to this meeting, with whom he thought he had a good relationship, and whom he admires a great deal, had not told him that he or she felt that way. "Is the teacher being a hypocrite?" the boy might wonder. "I didn't know that teacher felt that way about me."

Sometimes the "Claim of Shared Feelings" is a tag or a tail added to the report of an individual's report of feelings, frequently in an attempt to increase the significance and credibility of the individual's feelings. After a direct report of feelings of frustration and anger and resentment, I may say, "And I'm not the only one who feels this way" or "And a lot of other people are feeling the same thing" or "And the rest of the faculty feels the same way."

The third version of the Third Party Ploy I call the "Tobit Treatment." In the Bible, the book of Tobit narrates an incident when the elder Tobit went out in his courtyard and fell asleep next to the wall. He didn't notice that there were sparrows on the wall, and he did not cover his face when he lay down to rest. Some droppings from the sparrows fell into Tobit's eyes, and he began to go blind. In a very short time he could see nothing at all.

Similar to the "Claim of Shared Feelings," the "Tobit Treatment" happens when someone purports to report the feelings of unspecified people. "I just thought I ought to warn you that there are a lot of people on the faculty who are angry about your decision to change the schedule." "I don't want to mention any names, but there are some people who are not very happy that you're here." "Go easy on expressing your opinion, because there are some people here who are suspicious of you already." Such statements are like the bird droppings in Tobit's eyes.

The person making these statements has made it difficult for you to see clearly by clouding your perception with such warnings. You will walk blindly among the unspecified others, never knowing if or when you will trample on others or step into traps others may have laid.

People use the Third Person Ploy for a variety of

reasons. Sometimes they sincerely want to help establish or mend a relationship between two other people. At other times they desire to hurt the one to whom the report is made. It may be a way to report one's own feelings obliquely: Instead of saying "I don't like what you've done," I say, "Some people are upset with you because of what you've done."

No matter what the intention, the use of the Third Party Ploy in any of its forms will lead to the failure of relationships, not to their success.

Eight

"I Didn't Mean To . . ."

May 20th—Conversation at the Ferguson household:

"I'm not inviting her to Bill's graduation party," Dan Ferguson told his wife, Jean. "She passed me in the corridor last week and wouldn't even give me the time of day. She's been acting cold ever since. I'm sure our Bill will invite her son, Jamie, because they've been friends all through school. But I'm not including his mother. I don't know what she thinks I did to hurt her, but she's sure taking it out on me."

"Dan, you can't do that. Yvonne has been our friend since Bill and Jamie were children. Next year when Jamie graduates, you'll certainly expect an invitation from her. Besides, you don't even know for sure that Yvonne is angry with you."

"Oh yes I do. She walked right past me in the corridor and wouldn't even say hello. She's mad about something."

June 3—Conversation at the Nordstrom household:

"Jim, did Dan and Jean say anything to you about coming over to the graduation party they're having for Bill?"

"No. Since when do we need an invitation to go over to the Fergusons? Jamie is over there right now. I thought we'd walk over after things get going a bit."

"Well, I'm not so sure we're welcome. Dan has been acting strangely in school the past week or so. He hardly speaks to me in the faculty lounge. He always seems to be in a hurry to get somewhere else when I come in."

"Oh for crying out loud, Yvonne! You're imagining it. It's been a hectic time for all of you teachers these past two weeks with the school year coming to a close. He probably just had a lot on his mind, like you did."

"Just the same, I don't feel comfortable going over there without an invitation. You go if you want to, but I'm staying home."

June 3rd—Evening conversation at the Ferguson household:

"I told you she was mad about something."

"Daniel!"

"Well, Jim comes over and drinks up my beer, and brings a card for Bill, and stays around for less than an hour and goes home. Yvonne didn't even show up. I told you she's mad. The least she could have done is come over for Bill's sake. She taught him for the past two years! I don't know how she gets the idea she's better than everybody else."

"Jim told you she wasn't feeling well—a headache and upset stomach."

"Sure he did. And when Jamie heard his dad say that, he said that his mother had been all right an hour earlier. I tell you, Jean, I'm sick and tired of her 'better-than-thou' attitude. I suppose she thinks her little Jamie is so much better than our Bill. It makes me mad the way she treats us."

June 3—Late night conversation at the Nordstrom household.

"Geez, I felt funny telling Dan and Jean that you were sick. Why couldn't you just have gone over for a little while? They both wondered where you were, and I could tell that they didn't believe me when I told them you were sick."

"I didn't ask you to lie for me."

"I know, but what was I supposed to say, 'Yvonne is pissed at you and won't come over'?"

"I'm not angry with them. It's Dan. He's avoiding me. What do you expect me to do, go over there and be ignored?"

I won't prolong this any further; it's painful to make it up and write it down. Almost anyone is familiar with the kind of situation that has developed. From their own experience they could write the on-going saga of the ensuing feud between the Fergusons and the Nordstroms.

The story could end in any number of ways, but none will be very satisfying for the Fergusons and the Nordstroms unless something happens that invites them to check out their interpretations of each other's behavior.

No matter how the story ends, it began with Yvonne walking past Dan without speaking. Dan feels slighted, hurt, puzzled and angry. Feeling as he does, he assumes she intended "to make him feel" that way. The interpretation Dan gives to his perception of Yvonne's behavior generates his feelings. Failing to recognize this, Dan easily assumes Yvonne intended to cause him to feel as he does.

We tend to want to balance the effect someone's behavior has on us with that person's intention. If I feel hurt, I assume the other intended to hurt me. If I interpret someone's actions as unfair, and therefore feel angry, I assume that the other person wanted to act unfairly, and even did it in order to make me angry.

I also want to balance positive feelings with another's intention. If I feel happy because someone acknowledged me in a corridor, I assume the person wanted me to feel happy. If I feel appreciated because someone said thank you, I assume the person wanted me to feel appreciated. If I feel proud of what a son or daughter or a student of mine accomplished, I assume that person wanted me to feel proud.

In fact, I don't know what a person intended by his or her behavior unless that person tells me. I cannot perceive another's intention. I can only surmise what it might be.

If I cannot do more than surmise an intention, it is equally true that the other person does not know how I interpret what I perceive of his or her behavior. Since my feeling depends on my interpretation, it is doubtful, in most instances, that the other person intended that I should feel anything!

In certain instances, one person can behave in the hope that another will feel a certain way. A deliberate intention to influence the way someone else feels and possibly the way he or she behaves can be regarded as manipulative.

For the sake of trying to understand the example of Dan and Yvonne as a way of exploring the dynamics typical of much human behavior, I would like to distinguish "first instance" and "second instance" human interactions.

First instance interactions include the rather simple internal transaction from perception to interpretation to feeling to decision to externalizing the decision in behavior by two participants in an event.

The first instance in the example of Yvonne and Dan occurred when Dan perceived Yvonne walking past without a greeting, he interpreted that as a slight, he felt hurt, decided to avoid further unnecessary contact with Yvonne because he didn't want to be hurt again and carried out that decision by his behavior.

In first instance interactions, the initial behavior could quite possibly take place for a lot of reasons. Yvonne could conceivably have meant to slight Dan; she could also have not seen him because of her own preoccupations. The behavior could have been done without Yvonne's intention having any reference to Dan at all. Because Dan feels hurt, however, he assumes Yvonne intended to hurt him.

Dan's first instance mistake: He assumed he knew what Yvonne intended. Because of his assumption, he chose behavior designed to avoid further hurt. In that way he hopes to frustrate Yvonne's intention.

The first instance also includes Yvonne's perceiving Dan's behavior of avoiding her, which she interprets in such a way that she feels hurt. She wants to avoid further hurt, so she decides to behave in such a way as to avoid further contact with Dan.

Yvonne's mistake in the first instance is to assume Dan intended to hurt her by his behavior.

If Dan had been a skilled enough participant, he could have noted Yvonne's behavior. He could have been aware of his feeling and checked out his interpretation to see if there were other possible interpretations for Yvonne's behavior.

If Dan were a skilled enough participant, he could have decided he wanted to maintain a cordial and even friendly relationship with Yvonne, and he could have chosen to speak to her about his perceptions, interpretation and feelings. But he did not want to maintain a relationship with Yvonne; he wanted to avoid being hurt any further.

Had Yvonne been a skilled enough participant, she could have noted Dan's behavior as she perceived it. She could have noted her feelings and checked out her interpretation.

If Yvonne had wanted to maintain a cordial and friendly relationship with Dan, she could have chosen behavior designed to achieve that end. Instead she wanted to avoid further hurt and chose behavior designed to achieve that.

If the question had been put to either of them, both would have probably told themselves first, and then anyone who asked, that they did want to continue a good relationship with the other. Each would have assumed that the other did not want the good relationship to continue. In the first instance, each would have blamed the beginning of the breakdown of the relationship on what the other intended!

In fact, the relationship that had existed for years, as well as the relationship that was beginning to deteriorate, resulted from the behavior each of them chose.

I suspect most of us wish for a lot of things we take no behavioral steps to achieve. We tell ourselves that we wish we had a good relationship with other people. But we want to avoid the possibility of being hurt, so we don't choose to behave in such a way as to bring about the state of affairs we wish existed. Instead, we choose behavior which brings about the situation we want.

Because both Dan and Yvonne chose behavior that could achieve what they wanted, and because each of them assumed they knew the intention of the other, the affair moved to the "second instance."

Second instance differs from first instance in two ways: 1) the second time around, any perception is interpreted as confirmation of the assumption about the other's intention generated the first time around; 2) a pattern of behavior is chosen in order to cope with what one is now convinced is deliberate intention. A defensive attitude characterizes second instance interactions.

In the framework of the "Sometimes Useful Tool," the shift from "first instance" to "second instance" looks like this:

Fig. 8

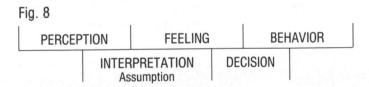

In the first instance something is perceived and interpreted on the basis of an assumption, which generates a feeling. Motivated by the feeling, one chooses a behavior.

Because of the mistake of assuming someone intended the perceiver to feel a certain way, the interac-

tion moves to "second instance." The original interpretation on the basis of the assumption is reinforced
and fixed in place as a means to interpret any further
perception. The feeling and the assumption unite to
form an attitude. Recall that an attitude is a decision
about how life is or ought to be and has both a cognitive and an emotional component. The cognitive element in the newly espoused attitude is the previous
assumption; the emotional element is the feeling generated by the previous interpretation.

Fig. 9

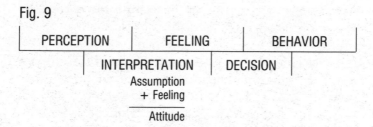

An attitude in the interpretation compartment will
affect interpretations of further activity. Further perceptions interpreted through the new attitude generate defensiveness.

In the example of Dan and Yvonne, Dan perceives
Yvonne's behavior of not coming to his son's graduation party and interprets it in such a way that it confirms
his earlier assumption that Yvonne wanted him to feel
as hurt as he had been feeling. He now feels angry, so
he decides to choose behavior designed to cope with
Yvonne's presumed intention to be hurtful by punish-
ing her for her "evil intention." He feels justified in his
behavior because he regards himself as a good person
who has been wronged by a less worthy person.

In the second instance Yvonne perceives Dan's behavior of not inviting her to the graduation party and she interprets it in such a way that it confirms her earlier assumption that Dan wanted her to feel as hurt as she had been. She now feels indignant, so she decides to choose behavior designed to cope with Dan's presumed intention to be hurtful by retaliating against the "unjust attack" she experiences from Dan. She too considers herself justified in this behavior, because she regards herself as a good person who has been wronged.

In this second instance Dan wanted to punish Yvonne and he chose behavior designed to do so. If he were asked, he'd probably claim that he wanted to maintain a good relationship with Yvonne but that doing so was impossible because of Yvonne's "evil intentions." In fact, although Dan may wish he were on good terms with Yvonne, he no longer wants to be on good terms with her; he wants to punish her. But he may remain unaware of what he wants.

In this "second instance" Yvonne wanted to retaliate against Dan's hurtful behavior. She chose behavior designed to do so. She probably remains convinced that she wants to be Dan's friend, but that Dan makes that impossible because of his "bad will." In fact, although Yvonne may wish she and Dan were still friends, she no longer wants to be Dan's friend; she wants to hurt him. But she may not allow herself to become aware of what she wants.

Both could remain convinced that the relationship was deteriorating to the point of loathing each other because of what the other intended, not because of what they themselves wanted or because of the behavior they chose in order to achieve it.

In the "first instance" neither party meant what the other assumed he or she intended. In the "second instance" both parties wanted to do what the other had assumed he or she had intended in the first instance.

Had either party wanted to pursue the cordial relationship instead of wanting to avoid further hurt, he or she could have asked the other what was intended by the action which was perceived. The matter could have been resolved by the simple statement: "I didn't mean to. . ." In the "second instance" the resolution is not nearly so simple. Each meant to hurt the other. The resolution of a second instance conflict can be achieved only by a repudiation of the pattern of behavior chosen to cope with the other's presumed intention, accompanied by an apology and forgiveness.

Second instance resolutions are not easily achieved unless a person is skilled at self-awareness. A person may wish a relationship were cordial and at the same time want to punish the other and choose hurtful behavior. "I didn't mean to . . ." would be a lie if a person had, in fact, wanted to hurt the other. Resolution of a ruptured relationship that has reached "second instance" can be achieved only when a good person admits that he or she has done something bad and can say to the other person, "I meant to, but now I'm sorry."

Assuming an equation between what one feels and what another intended pushes human interactions from "first instance" to "second instance." To disclose to someone what one is feeling in response to what the other has done and to ask what he or she intended is difficult, but it is the way to keep human interactions from getting to the level of "second instance." Human interaction can remain at a "first instance" level by ascertaining what the other meant and believing the person when he or she says, "I didn't mean to . . ."

The skilled participant knows it is a mistake to try to equate his or her feelings with another's intention, whether the feelings that are generated are "negative" or "positive."

Having belabored the example of Dan and Yvonne, I would like to examine a situation in which the feelings generated were positive. The same mistakes in human interaction can derail the possibility of human connectedness in pleasant situations.

I sat down at lunch one day and the conversation turned to the books I have written. Gary, one of my brothers in the Order, said, "You'd be surprised how often I have used your books." He proceeded to narrate examples of using my books in workshops he had conducted with college students and with divorced people. I heard his narration but had not perceived the events.

I interpreted Gary's narration as complimentary. I felt pleased. I decided to thank Gary and did so.

I did not try to equate my feeling with Gary's intention. I did not tell myself Gary wanted me to feel pleased; he may have supposed I would be pleased but his intention was simply to tell me that he found them helpful. I did not tell myself that Gary was trying to influence my feelings and perhaps my choice of behavior at that time or in the future. It was a simple "first instance" interaction.

I could have complicated this "first instance" interaction by telling myself Gary intended me to feel pleased. The next time I felt pleased at something

Gary told me, it would have confirmed my previous assumption about Gary's intention. I could then have chosen a pattern of behavior designed to cope with what I am now convinced is Gary's intention. I could have decided to act toward Gary in such a way, and only in such a way, that his feelings toward me remain positive and his behavior toward me continues to be such that I can feel pleased. I could choose never to do anything which might displease Gary or induce him to behave toward me in any way other than a way I would find pleasing.

Another way I could move to "second instance" interaction might be to reject as not-quite-true all statements from Gary that pleased me. I could dismiss them as simply Gary's way of behaving because he wants me to feel pleased.

I believe it is desirable to keep human interactions at the level of "first instance." A skilled participant finds it relatively easy to report to another what he or she is feeling and to ask if the other intended for him or her to feel that way. A skilled participant may at times—in dealing with certain individuals—decide it is wise to adopt a pattern of behavior designed to cope with the presumed intention of another. If he or she does so, the skilled participant has adequate self-awareness to know he or she is doing this.

A man I regard as a skilled participant, a chief executive of a small business operation, tells the story of having made a decision that displeased one of the junior management people in his organization. In an effort to punish the chief executive for the decision, the junior manager decided not to speak to him and carried out that decision for six months. Unfortunately, the chief executive didn't notice the middle manager wasn't speaking to him. Because he had no perception to interpret, he didn't feel hurt. He didn't attribute to the middle manager any intentions at all. Some months later when the middle manager came into the executive's office to apologize for his behavior, the executive graciously accepted the apology and offered forgiveness.

Skilled participants realize they don't know the intention of people whose behavior they perceive and interpret. Consequently, they learn to *respond* to the behavior and not to *react* to the intention they presume people might have had in behaving as they did.

Nine

"What I Want . . ."

Awhile ago, I returned from a year's sabbatical in England at the beginning of July and travelled around Wisconsin and Indiana visiting friends until mid-August when I reported to my new job. In October, along with two other friars, I was to take part as a facilitator in a meeting of one of our larger communities.

I was Jerry's passenger as he drove to Detroit for the meeting. During the drive over that stretch of I-94 that I have always found so boring, our conversation ceased and I lapsed into a reverie.

I imagined what it would be like to see the friars and other friends in the Detroit area, whom I had not seen since I left the administrative position that had earned me the sabbatical. As different people came to mind, I imagined what my conversation with them would be like after more than a year of not having seen each other. All these fantasized reunions were warm and cordial except one. I realized there was one person in Detroit I was not looking forward to meeting again.

I imagined this person throwing out some sort of jibe and my uncomfortable response. In my imagination I recounted what I had told myself many times during previous interactions with this individual. "I have never been able to connect in any but a superficial way with you. You seem so interested in your own image that you have never been able to become interested in anything about me." And so on.

From this imagined reunion my reverie shifted to two other people toward whom I had similarly negative feelings. Once again I was confronted with the realization that I had still not put to rest my anger about the way some people dealt with me while I was in administration.

On at least two previous occasions I had said to Jerry, "I think I need help dealing with angry feelings left over from my days in administration." But we never followed up on my desire to sort out what was going on inside of me.

As we continued on our way to Detroit, I thought again of asking his help in sorting out my anger. Without saying anything out loud, my reverie switched now to what my conversation with Jerry would be like when we finally got around to having it.

"I need some help in dealing with my anger. I'm still angry with some people even after a year's sabbatical," I imagined myself saying. And I imagined Jerry saying in response, "What are you getting out of still being angry with them? You must be getting something or you wouldn't continue to harbor those feelings."

"Well, it's one way of making sure I never have to

do administration again," I said, still only in my imagination.

My reverie ended abruptly as I slapped the dashboard and said out loud, "That's it!" I filled Jerry in on what I had been thinking. Then I said, "I'm holding a few grudges so I can feel justified in saying to anyone who might ask me to take another position in administration, 'No, I can't. See how scarred I am from the last time! I still haven't resolved some of my anger from when I was in administration before.'"

When I recognized my behavior—holding a grudge—I could see what I wanted—not to be asked to take any more administrative positions. I couldn't understand my behavior until I knew what I wanted. I came to know what I wanted by looking at and recognizing my behavior.

The relationship between behavior and what one wants—and the process of coming to self-awareness of these two realities—is a bit like a dog chasing its tail. My own awareness and understanding of my behavior increase as I get more in touch with what I want. And I recognize more clearly what I want by becoming aware of my behavior.

Several weeks or maybe even months after my return from Detroit I fully understood what I wanted to achieve by holding a grudge. I not only wanted to avoid administrative positions; I wanted to avoid being asked to take such positions. The behavior I had chosen was not necessary or even effective in attaining the goal of avoiding administration. That could be achieved by simply saying, "No, thank you" if such a position were offered. I wanted to avoid being asked because I know I find it difficult to say no when I'm asked to do something.

Because I find it difficult to say no, I preferred to spend a lot of energy holding grudges. It takes quite a bit of energy to hold a grudge. In order to stay angry I had to tell myself and possibly others how wronged I had been. I was more guarded in my relationships and less than cordial toward those I knew had behaved in ways that had caused me pain and those I imagined could behave that way.

As a result of my reverie on the trip to Detroit, my self-awareness increased significantly. I began to see what I wanted and how I had behaved in order to get it. I was now in a position to examine and to pass judgment on the appropriateness of both my intention and my behavior.

I rejected both as inappropriate on the basis of principles I have espoused as to how I want to live. I rejected holding a grudge as too much uselessly spent energy to make myself unhappy. I rejected my intention to avoid being asked to do more administration because I recognized I was trying to control how other people would behave. I wanted to manipulate others into not asking me to do any more administration.

Somewhere between October on that trip to Detroit and the January of the following year a lot resolved for me. I was asked to take another administrative post and I accepted it.

Yes, there is a moral to this story, actually four of them. They all concern knowing what one wants and choosing behavior designed to get it.

1. It is important to be aware of what one wants.
2. One will always behave in ways designed to get what he or she wants; therefore one can come to awareness of what he or she wants by recognizing one's behavior.

3. Behavior is always chosen from among the options open to a person.
4. When what one wants depends on the activity of others, the appropriate behavior is to request it directly.

The first point is this: It is important for a person to know what he or she wants. Unless one is aware of what one wants, he or she will not understand his or her behavior and in fact may not even recognize how he or she is behaving. Behavior is going to have consequences, whether or not one recognizes that behavior. A person unaware of his or her behavior will still suffer the consequences. But instead of recognizing the consequences as the result of one's own behavior, the person will feel he or she is the victim of circumstances over which he or she has no control and for which he or she is not responsible.

In the case of my holding a grudge, I initially did not know that I wanted to avoid being asked to do any more administration. As a result, I didn't understand why I was holding a grudge. In fact, until the trip to Detroit, I didn't recognize that I was holding a grudge. Nonetheless I suffered the consequences of holding a grudge. I was unhappy, less amiable to many people, speaking to them rarely and speaking about them regularly in negative ways. I recalled past hurts and imagined future ones. I was not as happy as I once was. These were all consequences of my behavior of holding a grudge as a means of getting what I wanted, but I didn't recognize them as such. I felt instead I was the victim of having been in administration. I told myself I had no control over these things and was not responsible for the unhappiness I suffered. Recognizing what I wanted was an important first step for me to extricate myself from the unhappy state into which I had put myself.

The second point is this: One will always behave in ways designed to get what he or she wants; therefore one can become aware of what one wants by recognizing his or her behavior.

For me the initial unravelling of my malaise came when I imagined Jerry asking me why I was behaving the way I was. Up to that point I didn't even recognize that I was behaving in any particular way. When I could see that I was holding a grudge, I could imagine Jerry asking me—or I could ask myself—what my behavior was designed to accomplish. I wouldn't be holding on to past hurts if I weren't getting something I wanted out of it.

The third point is: Behavior is always chosen from among the available options. I always choose my behavior, no matter how fervently and frequently I tell myself and others I have no choice in the matter. About many things I have no choice. I always have a choice about my own behavior. The truth of that assertion becomes more evident to me when I use the "Sometimes Useful Tool" to sort out my inner experience.

We have already seen that perception generates emotions because of the way one interprets what he or she has perceived. Frequently the process moves so spontaneously from perception to interpretation to feeling that it seems automatic. It takes some practice in self-awareness to recognize that interpretation, not perception, generates feelings. For instance, the sight of a snake generates almost instantaneous fear in many people. Few recognize that the reason for the fear is not the sight of the snake, but the interpretation that the snake is dangerous.

The presence of emotion in the circuits of my psyche moves me to action. I jump at the sight of a snake before I have even verified that I saw a snake. The internal process from perception to interpretation to feeling seems to proceed automatically to behavior.

But just as the transition from perception to feeling is not automatic, so neither is the transition from emotion to behavior. Between perception and feeling, interpretation intervenes; between feeling and behavior, decision intervenes.

In my imagined conversation with Jerry, he asked me in effect, ''Why have you decided to hold a grudge and what do you hope to get because of that behavior?'' Only after I recognized I was holding a grudge could I recognize I had chosen to do so as a means of getting what I wanted.

Often the intervention of decision is not allowed to operate on a reflective level. Habit, impulse or reflex seems to by-pass any chance to make a considered choice about how one will behave. In such instances, we rely on decisions made previously and our psychic system goes into action.

Return to the example my friend Marlene used. The apparently automatic transition from having her foot stepped on to feeling annoyed to speaking harshly to the perpetrator of the act soon appeared not so automatic when she saw the man's dark glasses and the white cane. Her new feeling in response to the same incident was one of embarrassment; her spontaneous inclination to behavior was an attempt to apologize. Upon being told that the man was only pretending to be blind, her feeling was one of anger and her inclination to behavior was to chew the man out or slap him.

In this scenario, the perception actually changed each time. The initial experience included only her foot being stepped on and being bumped into. The second experience included seeing the glasses and cane. The third experience included hearing someone else tell her about the man's intention in stepping on her foot.

However, should Marlene have her foot stepped on again, several interpretations will leap immediately to mind, and several feelings will vie for dominance. Most likely all action will be suspended until the perception and the interpretation are verified.

The possibility of choosing one's behavior does exist, even when great emotional charges run through the psychic circuits. Emotion prompts us to action; decision determines what action will be taken. We can choose our behavior from the several options open to us.

It is important to decide how one wants to live prior to any particular stimulus that calls for a response. One may still choose behavior contrary to the principles one wants to espouse. But should a person choose to behave contrary to one's general choice of behavior, the possibility exists for an honest critique of that individual behavior in light of something other than its effectiveness in getting what one wanted at the moment. Because of such ethical decisions, one can experience guilt, repentance, regret and reconciliation.

My espousal of the decision never to use the "Third Party Ploy," for instance, is an example of putting into place a decision prior to any particular instance in which I might be tempted to report to one person the feelings another has toward him or her.

Should I use the "Third Party Ploy" when I am charged with emotion, I can look back on my behavior and recognize I have done something that not only didn't work, but that I think is a poor way to treat other people.

The fourth point is this: When what one wants depends on the activity of others, the appropriate behavior is to request it directly.

During the drive to Detroit and for some time afterward, I thought I wanted to avoid administrative positions in the future. Gradually it became clear to me that I really wanted to avoid being asked to take such positions. The subtle difference between the two can be recognized if I am careful in asking myself what I want. When I say, "I want . . ." I need to listen carefully to what I mean by the next words. Do I mean to say, "I want to . . ." or "I want you to . . ."? The meaning of the words I say, not just the words themselves, needs to be attended to.

When I found I wanted to avoid being asked to take administrative positions, in effect I was saying, "I want you to refrain from asking me to do administration." What I wanted could come about only by the activity of others.

To try to get others to behave toward me in the way I want, instead of requesting that they do so, is manipulative and therefore inappropriate. Trying to get something from you without requesting it will mean that I do a considerable amount of positioning or pretending in order to evoke the response I want. I may indeed want you to trust me, like me, respect me, esteem me or behave in a way I desire, but if I decide to behave in a way designed to get that from you without your being free to choose how you will behave, I am manipulating you and most likely compromising myself.

Requesting is the only appropriate way to get what I want from others, but I may want something inappropriate. Turning again to the "Sometimes Useful Tool," it is inappropriate to request others to perceive things the way I do, to interpret things in a certain way and to feel certain ways. On the other hand, I can appropriately request others to want to decide and behave in certain ways.

I may, however, disclose to others that I want them to perceive, interpret and feel about things in a certain way. It would be wrong for me to request others to lay aside their own perceptions, interpretations and feelings and assume the perceptions, interpretations and feelings I would like them to have. But it is certainly acceptable for me to disclose to others that I would like them to perceive, interpret and feel the way I want them to. That is a self-disclosure, not a request. The skilled participant can recognize the difference in his or her self-awareness and can disclose accurately enough that the listener can clearly distinguish between self-disclosure and request.

I took the example I have used throughout this chapter from my own life and experience. I have access to my interior states as well as to my behavior. I can examine my perceptions, interpretations, feelings, wants and behavior. I can feel some confidence in analyzing the entire situation.

About the inner experience of others one can only hypothesize. The "Sometimes Useful Tool" is helpful in listening to the disclosure of others, however. I can perceive the behavior of others, but their perceptions, interpretations, feelings and wants I can only surmise unless they disclose them to me. Realizing I never know for sure what other people perceive, interpret, feel or want, I can still use the "Sometimes Useful Tool" to interpret what I perceive of their behavior.

I would like to give two more examples of what I heard from others as they spoke about what they wanted and how I saw them behave. I surmise from their behavior that they did not know what they wanted or at least that they did not want what they told themselves they wanted.

Ralph had worked in the boys' clothing department of a department store for almost seven years. He had been in line for promotion to assistant manager of the department but for personal reasons declined the promotion when it was offered. He remained a salesman on the floor.

After Ralph passed up the promotion and Mrs. Holahan was given the position, Ralph didn't socialize any more with the rest of the sales staff, although none of them knew why. Mrs. Holahan particularly was troubled by Ralph's new silence.

Mrs. Holahan confided to the rest of the sales personnel that she wished they would all do what they could to bring Ralph into the socializing that took place among the staff members. She said often that she wanted Ralph to speak to the others, but Ralph wouldn't even exchange greetings.

Mrs. Holahan did ask Ralph once if he would please communicate with her and the others on matters other than business. She told him how much she wanted that. Ralph said he'd try, but his behavior didn't change.

So far, so good. Mrs. Holahan said she wanted

Ralph to behave in a certain way and she had asked him to do so.

When Ralph's behavior didn't change, Mrs. Holahan spoke more frequently about how she wanted to have the good old relationship with Ralph that existed before he declined the promotion. She said she wanted this more than anything else.

One day Ralph came into the store at the regular time, but instead of walking immediately to one of the bays to arrange clothing, he nervously said, "Good morning." Mrs. Holahan responded with mock astonishment, "Well, it's about time." Ralph hasn't exchanged a pleasantry with anyone in the department since.

It appears to me that Mrs. Holahan didn't really want a good relationship with Ralph. Because of the behavior she chose, I surmise she wanted to punish Ralph for his behavior. She wished she and Ralph had a better relationship; but she wanted to punish him before she pursued that relationship. She didn't know she wanted to punish Ralph, but if she would recognize her response to his attempt to socialize, she could probably come to know she wanted to punish Ralph and then understand her behavior.

The second example involved an incident in high school. I was not present for the incident, but heard about it from a student in the class. Using the "Sometimes Useful Tool" I sorted through the experience with the student. He told about a teacher saying that for the final exam the class would not be responsible for material in several chapters of the book. The final exam did in fact have questions concerning the material in those chapters. The student considered that unfair and felt angry and mistrustful of the teacher. He said he wanted to trust the teacher again, but couldn't; he thought he was the victim of the teacher's behavior.

I asked him what behavior he could choose to deal with his anger and reestablish trust in the teacher. He agreed he could speak to the teacher. I coached him on how to express his perception as self-disclosure: "I heard you say . . . ; you did the opposite." He understood clearly how to disclose his interpretation of that perception: "I think that was unfair on your part." He also knew how to report his feeling directly in a non-coercive way: "I'm angry and I don't trust you anymore. That's painful for me." I heard him rehearse how he would disclose what he wanted: "I want to trust you." I heard him clarify what he was requesting of the teacher: "Would you help me deal with my painful situation by telling me what you remember saying and how you interpret what you did in the exam?"

Several days passed. I saw the student in the corridor and I asked him how his conversation with the teacher went. He hadn't talked to her yet. In the meantime, he found that all the classmates to whom he had spoken remembered the same events that he did, interpreted them as unfair and were angry. They also no longer trusted the teacher, and that was a problem they said they wanted to address.

A week passed. Still none of the students had spoken to the teacher. In fact, the rest of the school year went by and no student spoke to the teacher about the incident. Nor did I, under the rubric of avoiding the third party mistake.

I surmised the students wanted a reason to mistrust the teacher, not to dissolve their mistrust. I don't know their intention, of course, because they reported to me that they wanted to trust the teacher. But by speaking to each other many times about the incident and never speaking to the teacher they chose behavior designed not to reestablish trust but to continue and justify the mistrust.

All this would be complicated enough if we wanted only one thing at a time. But we have many wants simultaneously, and we have conflicting wants. I don't suspect that a skilled participant has awareness of all that goes on inside of him or her. Nor do I suspect it will be easy to sort out all the wants and desires one might have. I do think, though, that I can come to know the wants that prompt my behavior if I pay attention to that behavior. I also think I can understand my behavior much better when I know what I want.

_____ Ten_____

Behavior

By our physical presence and our behavior we insert ourselves into our world and influence it for better or worse. Our perceptions, interpretations, feelings and decisions coalesce to motivate and specify the behavior we choose, but of themselves they affect only our interior state. Behavior counts for something beyond the individual because it has consequences not only for the individual but for others. Other people perceive, interpret and have feelings about our behavior.

Behavior, chosen as a means of getting what we want, can be action or lack of action, speaking or refraining from speech. With the exception of involuntary bodily functions like breathing, sweating, blushing and digesting food, we always choose our behavior, however impaired our freedom, clouded our insight or minimal our awareness as we choose.

The habit many of us have of viewing our behavior from the inside out while everyone else views it from the outside becomes a major obstacle to personal connectedness. I am in touch with feelings that prompt me to some kind of behavior and with the intention that specifies the behavior I choose. I can be so conscious of my intention that I am unaware of the behavior other people see and hear so clearly.

Conversations recalled some time after they have taken place are good examples of how viewing one's behavior from two perspectives makes connecting with each other difficult.

"Hey, Father! You called me Jacob last night. How come?"

"Jason, I couldn't have called you Jacob. I've known you for two years. And I don't confuse you with any of the Jacobs on campus. I'm sure you heard me incorrectly."

"Oh no, I didn't. You said Jacob twice."

In this small and unimportant enough incident, I was willing to believe I had called Jason "Jacob." But I really don't remember having done so. I view my behavior from the inside out, and on the inside I know that the young man's name is Jason. Even as I called him Jacob, I was convinced I was calling him Jason because that was my intention. Jason, however, perceived my behavior from the outside. He could be mistaken about what he heard, but I am willing to believe his perception was more accurate than my own, because in his memory of the incident perception is not mixed with intention.

Expressions in our language can present a model for what the skilled participant will do in attending to his or her own behavior. "I heard myself saying . . ."

"I caught myself doing it again." "Before I knew it I had . . ." These expressions suggest one has viewed his or her behavior from outside of oneself.

Learning to perceive one's own behavior much as one perceives the behavior of others is a skill worth developing. One's self-awareness of his or her own behavior and one's ability to disclose that awareness helps one connect with other people, while awareness and disclosure only of what one intended to do can make connecting more difficult.

In any discussion of my behavior with others, it is extremely helpful to be able to see and hear what others have seen and heard of me. If someone wants to discuss my behavior with me, I will likely be in touch with my intention while they are in touch with my behavior. We will probably not connect in such a discussion.

Using the "Sometimes Useful Tool" the situation looks like this:

Fig. 10

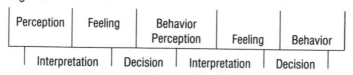

My own perception of my behavior enables me to critique my performance in the world. It does me very little good to intend all kinds of good deeds without performing them. It does me little good, for example, to approve honesty in speech if I rearrange and exaggerate details in my narration to such an extent that my stories amount to a pack of lies.

If I can view my behavior from the outside, I can join others in perceiving it. I can then find their perceptions more helpful in recognizing my own behavior. Viewing my behavior from outside aids my own self-awareness, and it increases the possibility of accurate self-disclosure. I can then more easily recognize what I want as I choose my behavior.

I will give one example, hoping the complexity of the process of analysis will not obscure the point I want to make.

I see my two friends, David and Mike, speaking with each other. As I approach, they break off their conversation. I recognize I feel worried at what I have seen. A bit of reflection alerts me to the fact that I am interpreting the conversation between two friends as detrimental to me because I assume they are speaking ill of me.

Fig. 11

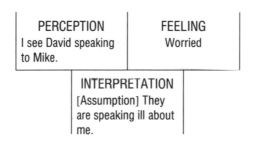

PERCEPTION I see David speaking to Mike.	FEELING Worried
INTERPRETATION [Assumption] They are speaking ill about me.	

My worry prompts me to some action. I tell myself I want to trust my friends. I tell myself how I want to feel and what attitude I want to maintain. To get what I want, I have several options: to speak to one of them directly, to speak to both of them directly, or to speak to neither of them. I decide to speak to neither of them.

Fig. 12

PERCEPTION	FEELING	BEHAVIOR
I see David speaking to Mike.	Worried	I remain silent.

	INTERPRETATION	DECISION	
	[Assumption] They are speaking ill about me.	I WANT: to trust them. OPTIONS: 1. speak to David or Mike 2. speak to David and Mike 3. *say nothing to either*	

I have chosen behavior to get what I want. In my own self-awareness, I am convinced that I remain silent because I want to trust my friends.

If I perceive my behavior, I can reconsider how effective it is in getting what I want. After a week of not mentioning to David and Mike that I saw them speaking and then breaking off their conversation when I approached, I begin to feel uncomfortable and embarrassed in their presence. A bit of reflection alerts me to the fact that I am interpreting my remaining silent as somewhat dishonest with my friends. I do, after all, espouse an attitude that says to trust one's friends means to be open with them.

My feelings of discomfort and embarrassment now prompt me to some behavior. I still want to trust my friends, I tell myself. So I reconsider the options open to me, and I decide to speak to David and Mike, telling them of my perceptions, my interpretation, my feeling, my decision and my behavior. I tell them further that having perceived my behavior, I interpret it as dishonest and therefore I feel uncomfortable and embarrassed in their presence, so I have decided to tell them the whole inner workings of my mind and emotions.

Fig. 13

A PERCEPTION I see David speaking to Mike.	C FEELING Worried	E / A-1 BEHAVIOR PERCEPTION I remain silent.	C-1 FEELING Uncomfortable Embarrassed	E-1 BEHAVIOR I speak to both.
INTERPRETATION [Assumption] They are speaking ill about me.	DECISION I WANT: to trust them. OPTIONS: 1. speak to David or Mike 2. speak to David and Mike 3. *say* *nothing* *to either*	INTERPRETATION [Attitude] I ought to be open with those I say I trust.	DECISION I WANT: to trust them. OPTIONS: 1. speak to David or Mike 2. *speak to* *David* *and Mike* 3. say nothing to either
B	D	B-1	D-1

[D-1 is the same as D]

If I view my behavior only from the inside, I may be so aware of my intention that I will not be aware of my behavior. I may be convinced my behavior is trusting because my intention is to be trusting.

My feelings of discomfort and embarrassment remain. I might try to understand why I feel as I do and even be willing to look again at my behavior of remaining silent to try to recognize what I am uncomfortable with and embarrassed about. But if I look at my behavior from the inside, it will be difficult, even impossible perhaps, to see how I am interpreting it. I will remain convinced I trust my friends, and will attribute my discomfort and embarrassment to what I perceive of their behavior.

Only if I look at my remaining silent from the outside will I be able to interpret it as something I perceive instead of something I intend. My feelings of discomfort and embarrassment alert me to the fact that I am interpreting my own behavior as less desireable than I approve. I can then reconsider what I want and, from the options open to me, decide to behave differently. I still want to trust my friends. But I decide now to speak to them both because I believe that behavior will achieve my intention to be trusting.

Neither the events of life around me nor my internal workings occur in the neat compartments of the "Sometimes Useful Tool." But with it I can more easily sort out the jumble of perceptions and interpretations, feelings and decisions, wants and intentions that swirl around outside and within me. I can do so with great advantage to the clarity of my self-awareness, the accuracy of my self-disclosure and the acuteness of my hearing what others disclose to me.

Eleven

The Skilled Participant

What does a skilled participant look like? He looks like a freshman boy, drawing pictures in my office with four of his classmates, who says to one of his friends, "If you'd give me the red marker I could complete this part of the drawing."

She looks like the woman in her mid-30s who says to her two partners in giving workshops, "I know you boys are tired, but before I return home tomorrow I want to go over the last segment of the workshop to see if there are any revisions we want to make."

He looks like the archbishop who writes in his column in the diocesan newspaper, "I guess I should not have been surprised to find that a group calling themselves Catholics United for the Faith decided to give the press a letter addressed to me which, unfortunately (or designedly?) arrived on my desk after the publication of its contents in the paper.

"The difficulty in responding is twofold: I resent being forced to dialogue publicly on inner-church matters in secular newspapers; secondly, I do not want thus to give the impression of recognizing this group as Catholic. It does not meet the requirements of the Code of Canon Law for Catholic associations with permission to form a chapter and function within the Archdiocese."

She looks like the religious sister who, to a friend's statement that his institution hires religious sisters at regular salary minus the taxes a lay person would pay, responds, "I object to your subtracting the amount of the taxes, because a sister pays taxes to her community to support the aging and infirm sisters."

She looks like the wife who can say to her husband, "I feel neglected because you have to spend so many nights at school for athletic events. I know you have to, and I don't resent your doing so. But I also know I'm feeling left out."

He looks like the young religious who can say to his formation director, "What you have just asked of those of us in formation seems grossly unfair. If I am ever in your position I will do just the opposite unless in the meantime I learn a lot that I don't know now."

He looks like the religious high school teacher who can say to a member of the junior class, "I like you. I presume you know I like you. But what I'm about to tell you does not stem from my liking you; it is my assessment of what I have seen and heard of you in the past three years. I think you have what it would take to be a religious. I think you would be happy as a religious and would contribute to any religious order you might join. I would like to invite you to join our order. I would like to live with you in community. I mean this

106

as no pressure; in fact I would hate to have you try to please me or anyone else in this matter. I mean this as an invitation only. But I do want to invite you to consider joining our order.''

He is the member of the board of directors who says in two sentences what the executive of one of the corporation's enterprises had just spent twenty minutes reporting, and the executive responds, ''I wish I had said it that well.''

These people look to me like skilled participants, because what they said to another or heard another say seems to indicate that they distinguish their self-awareness from their self-disclosure. They seem also to have distinguished clearly their perception from their interpretation, and both of these from their feelings and their desires. They did not attribute their feelings to those about whose actions they have their feelings.

Something was going on inside of each of the persons I mentioned above. The behavior each chose in response to his or her self-awareness was self-disclosure. They all chose behavior designed to get what they wanted: They chose to speak directly when they could have remained silent or spoken obliquely or behaved manipulatively.

In several instances the behavior cost the individuals considerably in terms of confronting other individuals. In each instance they refused to choose ''bargain basement'' behaviors—behaviors that cost less, but are ineffective or only partially effective in attaining what the individual wants.

To the best of my knowledge, only two of the people I mentioned above have ever heard of the ''Sometimes Useful Tool.'' The others may or may not have a conceptual framework by means of which they think and decide about how they will behave. But all are able to choose behaviors that will allow intimacy to grow between them and others.

Skilled participants benefit any group of which they are members because they have developed skills at self-awareness, self-disclosure and hearing. People vary greatly in their need and desire for intimacy. I don't mean to suggest that the more intimate relationships one has, the more perfect life will be; nor do I mean to suggest that the depth of intimacy achieved determines a successful relationship. I have convinced myself, however, that any effort to achieve a desired level of intimacy with whatever number of people one may wish will be successful to the extent that one is good at self-awareness, self-disclosure and hearing. I have also convinced myself that anyone who deprives himself or herself of all intimate relationships of any depth because of lack of desire or ability will be stifled in his or her development as a person.

I have presented my thoughts on the skilled participant for those who recognize in themselves a desire for more satisfactory relationships with others. In this final chapter I will summarize what I have written about the skills of self-awareness, self-disclosure and hearing.

A skilled participant recognizes that things don't just happen, but are the result of one's own or somebody else's behavior. In relationships with others, I don't point my finger outward toward others to identify the source of either pleasant or difficult situations. I know a basketball coach who said he can identify which of his players are winners and which are losers even before they play the first game of the season.

"The losers always point to someone else's performance to explain what went wrong with a play or a game. The winners look at themselves to see what they did poorly and could do better."

I am willing to develop behavioral skills at self-awareness, self-disclosure and hearing because I recognize that these skills allow me to let others know me. I allow others to know me, hoping that my doing so will be an invitation to others to let me know them.

A skilled participant recognizes that no matter how spontaneous the process from perception to feeling to behavior, that process is not automatic. Rather, I interpret everything I perceive, and I decide how I will behave. Therefore, I can respond to events, not simply react to them.

Recognizing that my feelings depend on my interpretation, I am slow to attribute to others the intention to "make me feel" a certain way.

As a skilled participant, I recognize that my awareness of events, persons and things is my self-awareness and that my speaking is not simply a narration of the way things are, but my self-disclosure.

I know that I am able to connect personally and in a non-defensive way with people whose perception and interpretation and feelings are very different from my own, because I recognize the limited nature of my perceptions and the subjectivity of my interpretations.

I distinguish between my perception and interpretation, both in my self-awareness and in my self-disclosure. I recognize that any awareness of and attempt to disclose my perceptions must be done by use of words that refer to the use of my senses; anything I am aware of and cannot express in a word that refers to my senses is something other than my perception.

The means by which I interpret what I perceive include opinion, assumption, attitude, bias, preoccupation and religious belief.

Attitudes include a cognitive and an emotional component. The skilled participant takes responsibility for his or her feelings to the extent they are generated by interpreting events on the basis of his or her attitudes.

The interpretation I give to what I perceive generates feelings that tell me what something means to me. I have feelings whether I acknowledge them or not, and they influence my behavior. The only constructive way for me to disclose my feelings is in a direct report. The difficulty of sorting out what feelings I have is compounded by the fact that I have feelings about my feelings.

While there is no morality to my feelings and I cannot change my feelings by willing to do so, my feelings are not unchangeable and I may have an obligation to change the interpretation which generates certain feelings.

A skilled participant will not report the feelings one person has about another to that other person, whether by simple statement, by the claim of "shared feelings" or by an indication that an indefinite group of others feels the same about an individual.

A skilled participant knows it is a mistake to try to balance the effect someone's behavior has with that person's intention. The skilled participant keeps interactions with others at the level of "first instance," inquiring about another's intention, not presuming he or she knows what another intends.

A skilled participant attends to his or her own behavior in order to understand what he or she wants. Knowing it is important to be aware of what one wants and that one will always behave in order to get it, a skilled participant always chooses behaviors from the available options. When what one wants depends on the activity of another, the skilled participant will request it directly, rather than try to get the other to respond in the desired manner.

A skilled participant perceives his or her own behavior from the outside in an attempt to be aware of his or her behavior and not just the intention that motivated the choice of that behavior.

The skilled participant is not a paragon of perfection in the matter of relationships with all others. He or she is a 13-year-old high school freshman who requests what he wants from others, a colleague who expresses her desires to her partners, an archbishop who distinguishes his responses from the intention of others, a woman religious who states her opinion frankly to a friend, a wife who reports her feelings in a noncoercive way to her husband, a young religious who discloses himself to his mentor, a high school teacher who knows he wants something of a student but who wants most not to manipulate that student.

The world is filled with skilled participants. Most of them have never heard of the "Sometimes Useful Tool." It remains my belief, however, that families, religious communities, boards of directors, diocesan pastoral councils, faculties of schools, and yes, even high school sophomore classes can have more skilled participants than they currently have. The increase in the number of skilled participants will come not from an increased amount of time these groups spend together but because individuals spend time with themselves developing skills at self-awareness, self-disclosure and hearing.